Portraits of Excellence

Principles of the Physics of Human
Behavior and Personality Functioning

by Isaac Hill

Tide Publishing
Toronto New York

Published by
Tide Publishing
Post Office Box 73538
Toronto, ON Canada
M6C 1C0

Copyright © 1998 by Isaac Hill

All rights reserved. No part of this book may be reproduced or transmitted in any form or by any means, electronic or mechanical, including photocopying, recording or by any information storage and retrieval system without written permission from the publisher, except for the inclusion of brief quotations in a review.

Printed in the United States of America

Canadian Cataloguing in Publication Data

Hill, Isaac, 1963-
    Portraits of excellence: principles of the physics of human behavior and personality functioning

Includes bibliographical references and index.
ISBN 1-894162-50-1

    1. Human behavior. 2. Self-realization. 3. Success. I. Title.

BF145.H55 1998   302   C98-900045-1

Table of Contents

1. Portraits of Excellence	5
2. Why Do We Need to Know?	11
3. A Physical Basis For Understanding Human Behavior	23
4. Need For Self-defense	39
5. Breadth of View	49
6. Need to Avoid Reality	59
7. Need For Others	65
8. Need to Be Greater Than Others	77
9. Need for Emotional Expression	87
10. Speed of Response to Motivation	93
11. Classification of Individuals on the λ_p Scale	101
12. Environmental Empowerment Factor	111
13. The Empowering Unit	121
14. The Motivation Vector	153
15. φ_p and Insecurity	161
References and Symbols	171
Index	173

Chapter One

Portraits Of Excellence

One of the greatest cravings of the human mind is the desire to be happy, blissful and satisfied. "The principal business of life," Samuel Butler wrote, "is to enjoy it."

Enjoying a fulfilling life is something we all want. We want everything within and around us to minister to and satisfy our needs in an ideal fashion, leaving us to relax and enjoy life. But our experiences seem to suggest that there are too many obstacles to achieving this goal—that a truly happy, self-actualized life may be impossible. Is it? If Yes, Why? If No, Why not?

It may be true that there are many obstacles to our happiness but where is our humanity if we cannot challenge our difficulties and turn them into opportunities? What is the use of our prodigious intelligence if we cannot find ways to make our life on earth comfortable and pleasurable?

6 Portraits of Excellence

The question of human happiness or fulfilling existence has exercised the minds of several philosophers and intellectuals down through the ages. Many theories and approaches have been proposed and the search for the answer continues to this day. The most basic and fundamental question in this direction has been: What is man and why does he behave the way he does? Once we can understand man and his behavior, we will be better able to discover and describe the pathways to human happiness since any solution must take into account the far-reaching springs of human nature. Mere diligence in beating about the bush will never do in a dozen years what a proper understanding of the principles of human life and excellence can in a day.

Relying on the personal opinion and unproven systems of philosophy of highly intelligent, successful people might have worked very well in the relatively quiet past but may prove ineffective or even disastrous in the more turbulent future.

Today, more than ever, we need reliable, concrete answers to the questions of excellence and the pursuit of happiness in a world of cascading physical and social change.

Such an answer, in this author's opinion, must lie in an impersonal portrait of human nature, not inherently subject to the changing emotions of men and women or the fluctuations in their outlook and taste. We cannot afford to allow our feelings come between us and the truth of our existence. We must be able to characterize human experiences and human behavior in terms that are not prone to biased, subjective reasoning. Only then can we arrive at the best way to understand behavior and design structures to produce and maintain excellence and happiness no matter which way the wind blows.

Instead of ploughing through pages and pages of personal history, opinions, unreliable experiments and sometimes unbridled boasting and brazen public opinion framing to

Portraits of Excellence 7

discover what might be useful to our condition, wouldn't it be much simpler, easier and more effective to take our lessons from an unbiased mirror which has nothing to gain, lose, hide or justify? This is the subject of this book.

Portraits Of Excellence is a graphic representation of human behavior in a portrait-like manner produced by referring behavior to its origin and observing it through its reflection in a physical "mirror." It is an application of the principles of physics (which have already been proven to be true in the physical world) to the science of human behavior. Besides being indispensable for sound social engineering design, such a portrait should be profitable to you as an individual reader in a number of ways:

1. Strengthen your self-confidence

Many life experiences as well as thoughtless remarks from others can make you feel uncertain about your worth and your abilities. With your self-confidence shaken you may be unable to develop your personality and talents fully, to take full advantage of your place in the universe. This book can help you see yourself more clearly and improve your self-confidence.

2. Turn obstacles into opportunities

The most reassuring fact of life is that we are equal to our needs. There is no problem, however bulging, tangled or complex, beyond effective human response. Obstacles will dog some of your steps in life. A better understanding of the root of your nature will help you turn these obstacles into opportunities.

3. Confront problems in a more relaxed and creative way

Knowing the parameters of your behavior will help you see your problems in a new light and show you how to confront them in a more relaxed and creative way.

4. Bring the full range of positive emotions into play

This book help you bring the full range of positive emotions—purpose, determination, hope, faith—into play in the game of life. With these on your side, you cannot lose.

5. A more courageous and fruitful life

Portraits Of Excellence will help you achieve a more courageous, happier and more fruitful life by bringing out the latent qualities you possess. You don't know what you have until you see them!

6. A practical set of tools

This book is designed to help you gain a practical set of tools to help you take effective action even when you fear that you may not be able to cope. The ability to do whatever it takes to be happy and fulfilled.

7. A useful change

The ability to change your life, to shape your perceptions, to make things work for you and not against you is one of the rewards you will gain by reading and understanding this book.

Portraits Of Excellence starts by answering the question: why do we need to know who we are and why we behave the way we do? It then proceeds to probe the foundations of human behavior and how to graphically represent this behavior through its reflection in a physical mirror. The remaining chapters provide more details on the portrait created in the course of the graphic representation.

Several analogies and descriptive metaphors are used in describing this portrait of human nature. A bit of imaginative, detached reasoning and an above-average intelligence may be required to understand this theory without being overwhelmed

Portraits of Excellence 9

by judgmental feelings. Our major objective here is to see human behavior as it is even if that means turning up parts of ourselves that we don't like to confront. Truth may be bitter but we don't do ourselves any good by hiding from it. Real progress in human happiness engineering must be based on the hard facts of human existence and nature.

All our discussions are derived by applying physics to the science of human behavior. We however avoided too much mention of physics to make sure the book is a social science text (which it is), not a course in physics (which it is not).

Scientific language is used throughout the text but every statement can be readily understood by non-scientists. Wherever scientific terms which may not be accessible to non-scientists are employed, they are immediately explained in more common terms. Conscious efforts were made to keep the discussions brief and to the point. Much more could be written on each subject covered but we decided to keep it short and sweet for easier comprehension and digestion.

We consider our job done if by reading this book you gain more practical ideas on how to empower yourself to live a happier, more fulfilling life!

Chapter Two

Why Do We Need To Know?

Evidence abounds that since the beginning of man, man has always been fascinated by the similarities and differences that exist between human kind. He has always tried to understand human behavior and to classify human beings into convenient categories based on their behaviors. There are several reasons for this. Some of these are:

1. Experience Calls For It

Dealing with human beings everyday one cannot but notice that there seem to be differences in human behavior and that these differences can be categorized into certain classifications. Some people are fast, some are slow; some are shy, some are bold; some are scrupulously honest, some take to dishonesty like a fish takes to water; some are gregarious, others are fine with the company of themselves; etc. In any given situation, people react differently to the same sets of stimuli.

So, generally people try to classify other people into some pigeonholes in order to know how to interpret and understand their behavior, how to deal with them and how to obtain what they want from them. How do they come up with the categories? Experience. More correctly, their own interpretation of experience.

On seeing someone, one almost instinctively tries to "place him" into one or the other category. And based on that categorization one proceeds to behave in a certain way towards that person. The problem, though, is that we find out all too frequently that our "instinctive" (gut feeling) classifications are wrong most of the time. But does that stop us from classifying people the next time we get opportunity to plan or evaluate our behavior towards anyone? Of course not. We yearn for an instant, sound method for reading people but in the meanwhile we continue evaluating and classifying people. This shows the depth of our desire to categorize in order to understand and effectively direct our actions.

2. Curiosity Asks For It

Men and women have always tried in one way or another to learn more about themselves and the world in which they live. Curiosity has driven us to probe the secrets of nature even when such knowledge might not necessarily have any practical application. We just want to know.

We want to know what things are, how they came to exist, why they are what they are and whether we may be able to change them to suit our desires.

We want to know why some people can survive tremendous difficulties while others dissolve under the weight

Why Do We Need To Know? 13

of everyday hurdles. Why people behave the way they do. What drives people to do good or to do evil. We want to know. We want to know what those tiny points of light in the sky called stars are. Why are they so many and why do they move across the heavens? What makes grass grow? Why are most grasses green? Why are people so different? What makes some people perform in areas where others cannot? Why? What? Why? How? and Which? We want to know.

Until a considerable body of knowledge is built up, many of our 'curiosity' questions cannot be answered in a manner we can consider reasonable. Primitive man could satisfactorily explain anything by attributing them to magic and to the influence of some supernatural power. But we are not primitive any more—we are now civilized men and women.

Curiosity is the main driving force of science and societal progress. Without curiosity man will be nothing but an empty sack of flesh subject to the world around him. Curiosity is the hallmark of our humanity, our consciousness and our existence. When man ceases to be curious he ceases to exist.

Man's curiosity has helped him tame wild and dangerous animals and made them obey and serve his purposes. By it man has conquered most of his physical environment and created for himself nice, comfortable surroundings in which the elements combine to minister to his welfare. By it he has conquered the oceans, the land and the space and with the constant improvement of science he can continue to be the king of this universe unless he fails to conquer the most important frontier of them all: himself.

Our curiosity impels us to ask such questions as:
• What is man?
• Why are people different?
• How many 'kinds' of people exist in this world?
• What determines each individual personality and behavior?

- How do we classify these personality styles and inclinations?
- How can each personality type be integrated into a community where happiness and fulfillment can be found for everyone?

We want to know.

3. Efficiency Requires It

Human societies are run by human beings and there are always problems demanding solutions. Man is always faced with the reality of his limitedness, his vulnerability and the uncertainty in which he is forced to live. So man devises means and mechanics to protect his existence. Most of these devices require the exercise of one gift or the other. Security operations require the ability to detect and prevent the activities of evil forces; planning requires the ability to envisage and analyze; selling requires the ability to tailor products and presentation to suit needs and personalities; etc.

Experience has shown that some people possess certain gifts while others possess other kinds of gifts. Experience also shows that there are different degrees of giftedness. Some are enormously gifted, some are moderately gifted and others barely have the gift in question. Some are excellent singers, some are good singers and some are—well—singers. Some are always coming up with original, brilliant ideas, some have ideas once in a while, some can only think when their backs are against the wall. Different degrees of giftedness.

Rosen, Crockett and Nunn (1969) noted that in a society, "it cannot help but be noticed that some persons make it while others do not. Though the reasons are often obscure, some people never seem to get started, others falter and run out of gas, only a few amply fulfill their early promise. Even in cases where there appears to be no marked differences in ability and where the starting point is roughly the same, there may be differences in eventual achievement" (pp.3-4).

Man is interested in knowing, if not actually predicting, who has what so that when a need arises he would know who to turn to. Every businessman wants a surefire way to identify the men and women possessing the qualities he needs without the often tedious and painful way of trial and error. He wants to hire the reliable, honest, able manager to manage the constant change that has become the order of the day in his business. How can he tell who to hire? This question is crucial because a mistake here could plunge his business (his means of survival and fulfillment) into oblivion.

Several personality profile tests have been developed and used in all human cultures. Every culture has one way or another of identifying, promoting and preserving the talents which its people find useful for their survival and meaningful existence. Psychological testing instruments are widely used in several establishments. Where no "formal" test instruments are used, informal "knowledge and experience" hold sway. No culture, business or establishment leaves the question of ability and giftedness to chance.

4. Intimacy Demands It

Man is a social animal. He needs to associate with other human beings in order to fulfil himself, to share his burdens, for companionship, for procreation and for safety. Yet he knows that not every human being qualifies as his mate.

Nature predisposes him to seek association with people who like what he likes, people who see things the way he sees them, people who do not find his natural inclinations offensive, people who understand his feelings, his actions and his dreams— people who can work with him to create a more enjoyable life and fulfil his dreams. For the majority of human beings, happiness is found almost exclusively in the domain of relationships. It is the most important aspect of our human experience.

16 Portraits of Excellence

Experience has shown man over and over again that human beings come in different stripes and through many failures and disappointments he struggles to be with the kind of people his spirit, life style and aspirations agree with. When he gets close to someone, he automatically begins to classify him into some kind of category experience has taught him to make of such human beings. He moves away from people whom he thinks are not his type to join a more congenial group. But all too often he finds that he has made a big mistake in the selection of his companions and he has to painfully start all over again seeking happiness in the company of his own kind. He yearns for a science that will help him unmistakably identify his true natural soulmates and avoid others whose behavioral language he neither speaks nor understands.

Susan Kolfa was 25 when she met Ron Harbord, then 29. She was a Physical Education teacher at a local high school while Ron taught Geology at the town's only university. Right from the day Susan met Ron, she was attracted to the handsome, young Assistant Professor but she noticed slightly something she was later to loathe deeply: Ron's seeming obsession with weighty matters and 'judgmental' analysis of every event, every issue under the sun. There was simply no room in his life for the frivolous, the fictional, for a relaxed atmosphere free from the 'burdens' of life. Ron had absolutely no idea that his excessive zeal for the serious side of life left his sweetheart cold (he thought every intelligent person loves to discuss and debate the important issues of the day).

Susan convinced herself that Ron would change; that she would help him discover and enjoy the softer side of life. They proceeded to get married. Seven years and two children later, Susan decided that she could not endure their unromantic, boring, "loveless" marriage any longer. Ron was doing very well in his intellectual enterprise, winning award after award for his brilliance and originality. He stepped up to his new stature as an intellectual genius and became even more rigorously intellectual and rational about everything than when Susan met him seven years ago. He was shattered to learn that his wife was leaving him; that she "even entertained" the thought that he did not love her. "Of course I love her," he protested. He just didn't know she needed him to spend "free" time with her and assure her of his love constantly. An example of an all-too-common mismatch of personalities.

5. Interdependency Needs It

Man is not capable of meeting all the demands of his existence alone. He depends on others to do some things for him. In the end everyone depends on everyone. And everyone wants to know the kind of person he is relying upon to do certain things for him. Can he fill the role? What will his work look like? Can I really trust him? What will happen if he fails to be who I think he is? And many times people are not who they seem. With the ever present need for others in everyone's life, there is a great need in everyone's mind to know just who the other guy is and how far or to what extent he can depend or benefit from him.

6. Personal Health Depends On It

Who am I? Why am I the way I am? Why do I like what I like and hate what I hate? Why am I different from the other guy? Why can't people understand me even when I speak plainly? Why do I keep falling into the same mistakes time and time again? Is there anything wrong with me? What path do I follow to find happiness and fulfillment in my life and work?

All these questions which affect a person's view of himself and therefore his psychological health (and consequently his physical well-being) drive individuals to go out of their way to find out who they really are. It is the rare individual who has not battled with some of these questions at one point or the other.

For their own health and happiness people want to know who they really are—to provide them with a handle for understanding the world around them and their own place in the universe.

Karen Matthews is a high-flying lawyer with several case victories under her belt; a very successful lawyer. With all her successes and good manners she still complains that people find her obnoxious, too argumentative, too opinionated, too quick to notice and criticize what others consider minor flaws. Is there anything wrong with me? she asks.

7. Simplicity Rides On It

As human beings, there is a limit to the degree of complexity our psychological system can tolerate. Consequently there is an incessant urge in every living person to simplify. This leads to model building and philosophical alignments of observed facts to simple wholes. This is why religion has so much appeal. It simplifies life by providing explanations and systems for explaining phenomena in simple terms.

This need for simplicity forces man to classify his observations of his fellow human beings into simple wholes which his mind can handle effortlessly. Here too is the root of over-generalization and prejudicial thinking.

8. Careers Depend On It

To be happy at work, it is necessary to find work that goes well with one's natural bent. Judith Barlow went to work for a large corporation as a computer analyst. After a few months with the company it started getting to her that she did not particularly enjoy the routine and impersonal nature of her job. She preferred dealing with people, not machines and lifeless numbers. She asked for a transfer to the Sales department. There she didn't have to use her computer training but she found more fulfillment, satisfaction and a much higher take-home pay (about three times what she was making before).

9. Effective Self-improvement Needs It

This is the age of self-improvement. Desiring to be everything we ought to be, we want to know what aspects of ourselves need to be changed, what can be changed, what should be left as is and what cannot be changed.

On TV, on the radio and in the print media—everywhere—there are gurus with neat, "proven" techniques or products that could help us transform our lives into exactly the model the society wants. They paint for us rosy pictures of what life would be like with a slim, beautiful body, how to develop a new way of talking across lines and amass wealth overnight, a pathway to connect with our deep self, how to obtain the creative brain power of Albert Einstein, Chinua Achebe, Karl Marx or even Jesus Christ in just five minutes, etc.

We have tried many of these programs and they didn't seem to work very well for us. Why didn't they work as well for me as they should have? They must be working perfectly for someone. See all the testimonials in the ads and the number of people using the product. Why not me?

10. Social Engineering Requires It

Every social improvement program or theory is based on certain assumptions or facts on the nature of human beings.

Plato believed that all men (i.e. all human beings) are not endowed equally with visionary wisdom so he proposed that for societies to enjoy peace and for its population to find individual happiness, wise men should bear rule (the Rule of the Wise). Jesus Christ preached that everyone needed to reconcile with God and be born again (because everyone's original nature is evil) in order to find peace.

Jacques Rousseau, Karl Marx and others were of the opinion that man is naturally good, that society (especially the capitalistic economic system) is to blame for man's inhumanity to man and other evils. So when the capitalist system is overthrown, man will be able to find peace and happiness in a classless, humanistic society.

None of the above theories (and others not mentioned here) have proven to be able to provide all the answers. We still need to search for and develop an objective knowledge of the human nature so that we may be able to design social structures and processes to suit the needs of everyone.

The Consequences Of Not Knowing

The consequences of not knowing who we are are many and dangerous. Some of them are:

1. Waste of Human Resources

Not knowing who each individual is, what he or she can do or cannot do, where and how he or she can contribute to the society, etc. will result in people being employed in jobs they are not suited for which in turn will lead to a waste of human intelligence, energy, time and effort. Imagine cutting a tree with a razor blade as opposed to a chainsaw. What a waste of time, energy and effort!

Ignorance of the true nature of man can also lead to disastrous social experiments. No matter how well intentioned a social program is, if it is not based on realistic assumptions or knowledge of the nature of man it is bound to leave devastation in its wake. Nature never excuses ignorance.

2. Relationship Disasters

Two people enter into a relationship to meet certain needs that are important to each individual in the union. The relationship succeeds or fails to the extent that each partner feels that his or her needs are being met. As we have seen, people differ in their natural inclinations, in their likes and dislikes. For a relationship to work there must be some degree of compatibility. Without understanding the true nature of man, it is difficult to determine who is compatible with who, other than by heart-breaking trial and error.

3. Anxiety, Confusion, Anger & Helplessness

Not knowing who one is (i.e. one's true nature) can lead to stress resulting from untoward experiences one is not able to understand, explain, or manage. This stress can lead (and has been known to lead) to anxiety (worry), depression, confusion, anger, and a feeling of being overwhelmed or helpless.

4. Friction and War

Because of not knowing who man is and what is in him, many individuals have tended to rely too naively and foolishly on individual experiences extrapolated to whole groups. If he is treated unfairly by one or two people from Glompeople, he believes that everyone from Glompeople are bad and therefore should be avoided. When these sentiments (which are really manifestations of human ignorance) are expressed by many individuals, a dynamic of group prejudice and hostility is set up which usually leads to friction, violence, unrest, fear, and ultimately to war.

So many wars have been fought and millions of our race have been destroyed for no other reason than that man has failed to understand the dynamics of his existence and has been groping in the dark to find happiness and fulfillment in a largely hostile world.

Man has been able to conquer most of the world around him, from the oceans to the skies, but he has failed to find himself and his real place in the world. The result is a frantic search for meaning and the invention of several theories and philosophies which purport to answer the question of man's existence. The evidence to date is that he has not been completely successful in his search. Several religions, each with its tabernacles and proofs of infallibility has claimed to show man the way out of the wilderness of meaninglessness to a meaningful and happy existence. In the end we have several religions, many different answers, so much confusion of tongues, and man is no closer to the answers he so desperately needs today than he was ten thousand years ago.

Chapter Three

A Physical Basis For Understanding Human Behavior

In this section we will be introducing a looking-glass analogy to help shed some light on the nature of human individuals. To bring out the foundational principles on which it is based, let's start by asking and answering three cardinal questions:

(1) What is human behavior?
(2) What drives human behavior?
(3) How do we create a looking-glass analogy of human behavior?

1. What Is Human Behavior?

An individual's personality or behavior is a hidden quality which is displayed or reflected in his or her actions. Every action is a form of motion. So behavior is reflected only during motion. Therefore, as a psychological entity, the human individual is a moving object. The motion of the "object" (in other words, the psychological characteristics of the individual) would be a function of:

    (a) The physical (i.e. natural) properties of the object

        The motion of a plate-like object would be different from the motion of a spherical object.

    (b) The force causing it to move in a particular direction

        A large force would move the object farther than a small force.

2. What Drives Human Behavior?

Our main business in life is to survive and enjoy everything that life has to offer. All our behaviors (everything we do) are created, directed, conditioned and limited by this grand desire.

We want to control the elements and circumstances around us to promote our survival and enjoyment of life. Unfortunately, we are very often not able to control everything around us to our satisfaction. Life is greater than us and does not yield to our every desire.

We want survival and happiness but we often get what we consider to be only a fraction of what we really want. This discrepancy between what we want and what we feel we are able to get creates something like a potential difference that generates a current of insecurity in us. Let's look at this potential difference from a physical angle.

A Physical Basis 25

From our elementary science, we remember that potential difference (voltage) is given as:

$$pd = I R \qquad (3.1)$$

where:
    pd   is the potential difference (voltage)
    I   is the current
    R   is the resistance to the flow of the current

The current of insecurity, I, created by the inequality of what a person wants and what he can get (potential difference, pd) given analogously in equation 3.1 is the secret driver of every human behavior. Every behavior of man is an attempt to respond to this insecurity and achieve full survival and happiness.

Insecurity here is defined as a feeling of inadequacy, a feeling that something is missing, that all is not alright, a feeling of need. We start feeling this insecurity or frailty very early in life. Born helpless into the world, we are, at birth, inadequate to meet our own needs for survival and happiness. We have to depend on others. This inadequacy decreases as we grow up and learn or develop survival skills but it never fully disappears. All through life we find that there is a disparity between what we want and what we can get.

Anything that affects our survival and/or happiness affects this discrepancy—uncertainties, hardships, hurdles, our perceived or real inadequacies and every other source of insecurity that put our survival and/or happiness into question (i.e. makes it vulnerable). Since we want to survive and enjoy our lives, responding to the current of insecurity becomes the main fountain of our behavior.

Notice in equation 3.1 that every body offers a resistance R to the flow of the current of insecurity, I. If R is large, insecurity will be smaller than if R is small, given the same potential difference. For example, if pd = 10 and R = 5, I = 2; for the same pd = 10 but R = 2, I = 5. R is a function of the nature of the material and the environment. Some materials naturally have low R, some have high R. The resistance of a given conductor usually increases slightly as its temperature is raised. Heat empowers the conductor and increases its resistance.

In the case of the human being, R is a function of the nature of the individual as well as the nature of his environment. Biologically, some human beings are more susceptible to the flow of the current of insecurity (because of lower R) than others whose higher R translates into weaker currents of insecurity in their lives. In other words, when human beings are exposed to the same potential difference (i.e. discrepancy between what they want and what they can get), they experience different levels of insecurity, depending on their R. This genetically determined R is the basis of the biological uniqueness of human behavior. The environment or condition in which an individual lives also affects R—the basis of the environmental factor in human behavior.

Individual psychological behavior is therefore predicated on the nature of two intertwined empowering sources:
        (a) Biology (genetics)
        (b) Environmental or social factors
Notice that 1(a) and 2(a) are analogous, and 1(b) and 2(b) are analogous.

3. How Do We Create A Looking-Glass Analogy of Human Behavior?

We have established two principles so far:
    (i) Human behavior is manifested in action which is a form of motion.

A Physical Basis 27

(ii) Human behavior is driven by the current of insecurity generated by the potential difference between what he wants and what he feels he is able to get.

Now we want to find a way to physically model the above principles of behavior. Why physical? We want a physical model because such models tend to simplify complexities and sharpen conceptual images. We have already seen how a physical phenomenon helped us visualize the driving force of our behavior. Other reasons for the physical approach will be discussed later in this chapter.

We need to find something in nature whose motion is determined by a sort of insecurity to model human behavior. Apparently everything that moves is driven by some sort of potential difference. A difference in temperature drives heat movement, a difference in pressure moves water, a difference in concentration leads to a movement of mass, potential difference drives electricity, etc. It is not surprising that we are driven like the rest of nature.

If we can find something in the physical world to model this insecurity we can learn more about human behavior from a "looking-glass."

Fortunately, we can. In the physical world, the motion of a particle is governed to a large extent by its "insecurity." We have seen that insecurity is produced by a deviation from the perfect condition. We saw that when what a man gets is less than what he wants, he feels a current of insecurity, a dissatisfaction with his life with respect to that incident. This insecurity affects his behavior in one way or another, all things being equal. The same sort of thing occurs in particle behavior. When a particle's shape deviates from the perfect shape, its behavior in motion is different than when its shape is perfect. We shall use this deviation from the perfect shape to model

28 Portraits of Excellence

human behavior. In other words, we are implying by this analogy that when a man cannot get what he wants, his feeling of insecurity is 'in a different shape' than when he can get what he wants.

A particle's deviation or lack of deviation from the perfect shape will define particle physical insecurity or lack of it for us. The perfect shape we shall be using in this model is the spherical shape and the measure of a particle shape's deviation or resemblance to it is called sphericity.

Before we continue with our discussion of sphericity, let's point out that we are assuming that particle size, d_P, and particle density, ρ_p, are equal in every case, leaving only particle shape as a variable for our consideration. Translated to our human model, we are assuming that all human beings are created equal, the only distinguishing characteristic, for our investigations, is the degree of roughness or smoothness of human behavior. It doesn't matter whether the individual is big or small, tall or short, green, blue or yellow, rich or poor, fat or thin, male or female; nothing matters except individual behavioral characteristics.

Sphericity is a measure of how much a particle's shape resembles the shape of a sphere. A perfect sphere would have a sphericity of unity (1.00). Particles that are less than perfect would have sphericities less than unity (0.01 - 0.99). We will denote this sphericity as λ_p. Particles of different sphericities behave differently in flow. For example, a particle of $\lambda_p = 0.91$ will respond faster (i.e. at lower velocities) and better than a particle of $\lambda_p = 0.15$ to pneumatic transport.

If a group of particles differ only in their shape characteristics (sphericity or λ_p), their behavior in motion will vary in proportion to their λ_p as depicted in Figure 3.1 (the lines may not be straight, curved or smooth in practice). Properties a, b, and c decrease with increase in sphericity while d, e, and f increase with increase in sphericity.

A Physical Basis   29

We are assuming that human insecurity is analogous to particle sphericity. A sphericity (λ_p) of 1.00 denotes perfection or total absence of insecurity. Individuals with λ_p of 1.00 would

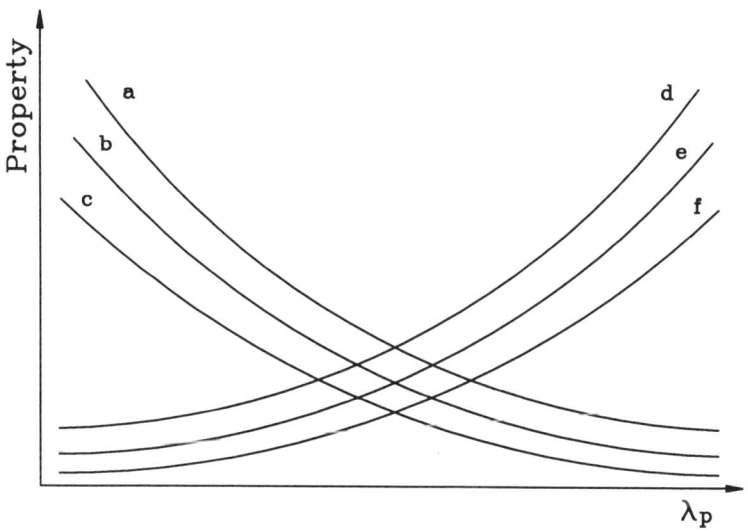

Figure 3.1. Behavior in relation to sphericity.

be perfect in their behavior; they would feel no discomforting insecurities that would drive them to do what is not right or perfect. They would always be in perfect harmony with their conscience, their behavior being never out of line with what is perfect, just and commendable. They would never know the discomfort that comes from doing something and later being condemned by their conscience. They would be perfect.

Individuals that are less than perfect would have sphericities (λ_p) less than one, any where from 0.01 to 0.99. They would feel insecure in varying degrees, depending on their λ_p. A person with a λ_p of 0.30 would be more insecure than one with λ_p of 0.72, for example. Since they are not perfect, their behavior will not always be perfect or in line with what is just and commendable.

You must have noticed that we are using particle sphericity here as we used R above. A high sphericity means a large R. When R is large or sphericity is high, the intensity of the current of insecurity is low, other things being equal.

The λ_p represents the behavioral characteristics that are unique to the individual (biological uniqueness), the characteristic behavioral bent or disposition bestowed on each individual by his genetic makeup, his natural self. As we saw before, it is better conceptualized as the natural resistance R to the generation of the current of insecurity by potential differences. When R is large, λ_p is high and insecurity is characteristically low. Sphericity is not built or acquired by the efforts of the individual or anything of that nature; it is his biological given.

Like the case of the particles discussed above, the psychological behavior of individuals will vary in proportion to their λ_p as depicted in Figure 3.1 (the lines may not be straight, smooth or curved in practice). Properties a, b, and c decrease with increase in λ_p while d, e, and f increase with increase in λ_p.

From Figure 3.1 you can see that this theory subscribes to the view that each behavior varies as a continuous function from high sphericity (λ_p) to low sphericity (λ_p) or vice versa. Human behavioral characteristics are not discrete functions—not an either/or proposition, for example, you are either creative or you are not. The question is how much of each behavioral characteristic the individual possesses. For example, every human being is creative but some are more creative in certain directions than others.

In other words, this model follows the trait dimension point of view. In trait theories, individual difference variables are seen as continuous, differing from each other in terms of the amount (quantity) of some characteristic that they have.

Bundles of Insecurity

"Part of the process of making things more manageable is identifying how lots of specific behavioral qualities may actually reflect a single trait that ties the behavior together" (Carver and Scheier, 1988, p.64)

In order to make our discussion of human personality simpler or more manageable, we will attempt to organize human behavioral characteristics into bundles of needs or behaviors driven by insecurity or lack of it. The following seven bundles will be discussed:
1. Need for self-defense η_{sd}
2. Breadth of view η_{bv}
3. Need to avoid reality η_{ar}
4. Need for others η_{fo}
5. Need to be greater than others η_{go}
6. Need for emotional expression η_{ee}
7. Speed of response to motivation η_{sr}

Their general variations with λ_p are shown in Figure 3.2.

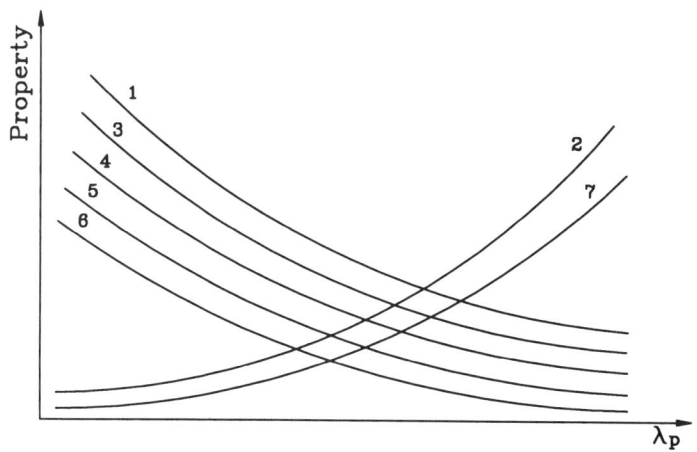

Figure 3.2. Variation of behavior with sphericity.

A separate (brief) chapter will be dedicated to the discussion of the content of each bundle. No experiments have been done on any of these traits by this author. Only general points to be verified later by experimental data are presented.

The Environmental Factor

Just as the physical characteristics of the particle do not determine everything about the motion of the particle, individual biological uniqueness does not tell the whole story of each person's psychological behavior. Remember that we saw that R has an environmental component since lower temperature decreases R and higher temperature increases it.

Another factor that affects particle motion is the momentum imparted to it by the medium (force) which is causing its motion. That force empowers the particle if it is in the positive direction with respect to the particle, thereby reducing its insecurity. If it is a contrary force (in the negative direction), it "disempowers" or "weakens" the particle, thus increasing its insecurity.

This is analogous to the empowerment—positive or negative—of the individual by his environment (the environment is where the individual interacts with the world and people around him; where he displays his natural psychological propensities). Some environments empower the individual decreasing the intensity of the current of insecurity he feels. Some other environments disempower the individual, making the individual feel a greater intensity of the current of insecurity.

The momentum imparted to the particle by its medium, as we will see, is a product of the interaction between the particle's nature and the characteristics of its medium. We shall call this product φp. For the individual (human particle), environmental empowerment or disempowerment is a product of his biological nature and the nature of his environment. We'll also designate this as φp. As we shall see later, certain aspects of an individual's φp can be improved or changed by the individual while other aspects are under the control of the society in which he lives.

In the next section we shall take a closer look at λp and the bundles of insecurity we identified. Later we will take up φp to complete the picture. After that we shall examine the implications of the portrait we have developed. In each case we shall be as brief as possible to allow us to grasp the essential elements of the theory without the grit of oratory.

Insecurity? Come On

This author knows how it must feel to know that our behaviors are driven by insecurity. He doesn't particularly like the finding that human behavior is driven by insecurity. How could it be said that all those powerful men and women in the society are driven by such an insulting characteristic as insecurity? Such a low reason should not be the cause of our treasured behaviors. It would feel much better if it is found that we are driven by nobler factors, by higher powers—that our behaviors are God-given or something like that. But unfortunately the verdict of reality, as we shall see, is that we are propelled by the insecurities connected with our desire to survive and enjoy what life has to offer. Truth, they say, is bitter but it is often good medicine.

One other problem with the fact that insecurity is at the root of human behavior is that professional psychologists and counselors will find it difficult to advise their clients that their life problems have their origin in insecurity. It is so much better and more appealing to people seeking relief from pain to learn that they can attribute their problems to other people, to the movement of some stars, to God, to some mysterious philosophy or something else. To tell them that a better management of their own insecurity is the key to the solution of their problems is to put extra demands on their already burdened life. Wouldn't that be cruel?

Benefits Of A Looking-Glass Analogy

Once we can relate human psychology to a particle in motion, we can visualize human behavior in a clearer focus than ever before. "Since finding out what something is is largely a matter of discovering what it is like," Jonathan Miller wrote, "the most impressive contribution to the growth of intelligibility has been made by the application of suggestive metaphors." This method will lead to an "impressive contribution" to the understanding of human behavior and personality functioning.

There are many other benefits of using this kind of physical model approach to study human psychology. Some of these are:

1. A Frame Of Reference For The Objective Comparison Of Data

If it can be shown that the particulars of particle motion are analogous to the contents of human behavior (which is one of the things we are attempting to show here), this can be used as a frame of reference for the objective comparison of data from different sources. When this model is fully developed and adopted by the scientific community we will be able to plot the results of several human behavior experiments in terms of λ_p and φ_p. Theories and data from different sources can then be compared objectively on λ_p and φ_p frames of reference.

2. Strong Basis For Problem Isolation And Solution

By delineating human behavior into λ_p and φ_p coordinates it will be much easier for scientists to isolate and solve personal and social problems. Looking at complex human problems through its more manageable reflection on a physical basis will simplify the task of problem identification and increase the likelihood that a solution can be found.

3. Good Way To Overcome Prejudicial Reasoning

It is natural for most human beings to feel that their lives (and that of their group) are models of the best in human behavior. With such inclinations hugging the mind of a scientist it is difficult for his theory or the interpretation he gives to his data to be without bias. By referring data to a physical basis which anyone can easily verify on his own, a large proportion of the prejudicial reasoning that has plagued social science for a long time can be overthrown.

4. A Looking Glass

It is hard, very hard, for a human being to see his own ears, eyes, in fact, most of his face except through the agency of an external body—a mirror, usually. In the same way it is difficult, very difficult, for us as human psychological entities to come to an objective knowledge of human psychology without the use of an external agency—something like a looking glass.

In this book, the use of a particle in motion as a looking glass is suggested. How this can be done and the type of general results we can expect are briefly demonstrated. Other animals may not be good candidates for a looking-glass analogy of human behavior because they are living things like us. While we can learn one or two things from them, we cannot see our picture in them as we can in a looking-glass analogy employing non-living things. The physical, non-living looking glass reflects our image as no biological entity can.

5. Impersonal Portrait Of Human Behavior

Science has to be impersonal in order to be progressive and effective in solving the problems we employ it to. As alluded to earlier, it is not easy to be impersonal when you are studying yourself. How can you separate yourself from yourself or stand outside of yourself looking at yourself without being biased? No one can undertake to study any aspect of human behavior without being personal about it. We can be objective once in a while, even more than 50% of the time but general objectivity cannot be assured. Further, there will be "scientists" hiding comfortably behind the facade of science to promote causes that are dear to them using fraudulent data. When we start to create impersonal portraits of human behavior by the methods outlined in this book, these fraudulent scientists will find it difficult to use science as a cover for their evil designs.

6. Better Visualization And Description

Human behavior is undoubtedly complex. By using the impersonal portrait proposed in this book we can "map" these large scale complicated phenomena on the social plane in simpler terms on the physical level—more like taking a picture of a large object and printing it on a small piece of paper you can conveniently hold in your hand or place on your table for further study. True, the picture is not the object but if it is good it can provide you with a good understanding of the object at less cost and hassle. In fact studying a picture of a complex object is often more instructive than studying the object directly.

By referring human behavior to a looking-glass analogy on the physical scale we can better visualize and describe the functioning of human personality. We will be better able to map or classify human behavior. In this book we have attempted to show how this better visualization can be obtained. You have to bear in mind, however, that this is a first attempt. More input will be needed for the entire picture to shine forth.

7. Better Understanding And Prediction Of Behavior And Performance

As we will see in the chapters ahead, the looking-glass analogy described in this book will lead to a better understanding and prediction of human behavior and performance because it looks at λ_p (biology) and φ_p (environment) as concrete variables. Other theories have tended to rely more on one of the two than the other. It also provides answers to previously unanswered questions.

8. More Useful For Social, Political And Economic Engineering

It is hard to extend fluid theories (theories without clearly defined reference frames) of human nature directly to social, political and economic issues. This theory is different.

38 Portraits of Excellence

We can easily extend this theory to isolate and solve social, political and economic problems by analogously treating society as a group of particles and comparing social dimensions to results obtained in particle-group dynamics. In fact this author has already done this and the analogy is functionally great (this is the subject of another book).

Chapter Four

Need For Self-defense

We feel insecure when there is a discrepancy between what we want and what we feel we can get. Since we never fully get everything we want, insecurity is always a part of our existence on this side of consciousness.

The need for self-defense arises from insecurity. It is an expression of our feeling of inadequacy in our unconscious or conscious mind, a feeling that we are vulnerable to forces outside ourselves. We want to be safe, so we can survive and enjoy our lives but we find that we are not in complete control of everything that affects our safety, survival and happiness. The potential difference between the perfect safety and survival we want and the vulnerability we experience creates a current of insecurity in us. This feeling of vulnerability results in a need to defend and/or protect oneself from attack or from dangerous situations.

When we are born into the world, we immediately realize that our survival is predicated on our ability to constantly meet the unending demands of life, some of which we feel we cannot successfully meet on our own. This feeling of inadequacy (the secret fear that we may not be capable of meeting all the demands of life) translates into a feeling of vulnerability. We know that our survival is at best precarious. Since we want to live and enjoy the wonderful springs of consciousness, we move to protect or defend our interests and fulfil our desire to live happily. The amount of investment we will bring to bear on this need will depend on how vulnerable or insecure we feel. If we feel very vulnerable or very insecure we will invest more into our self-defense than if we feel little or no insecurity. If we don't feel insecure or vulnerable at all, there will be no need for us to defend ourselves. So the need for self-defense arises from insecurity.

Everyone feels this need in one degree or another, unconsciously or consciously. For the same potential difference, people with a low resistance (R) or low sphericity will feel more insecurity and hence a greater need for self-defense than people with a high R or high sphericity. In other words, the need for self-defense will be highest at low λ_p and lowest at high λ_p. Please note that we will be referring to the two ends of the spectrum by low λ_p, lower λ_p, high λ_p, or higher λ_p interchangeably.

To examine this trait dimension further, we shall look at the following sub-level manifestations of it:
    1. Self-orientedness
    2. Inconsideration of others
    3. Need to be on guard
    4. Cunningness and tactfulness
    5. Deliberate faking
    6. Practical, present-oriented

The general variation of these need for self-defense manifestations with λ_p are visually represented in Figure 4.1.

Please note that the different headings are meant to describe one overriding characteristic so there would, naturally, be overlapping statements.

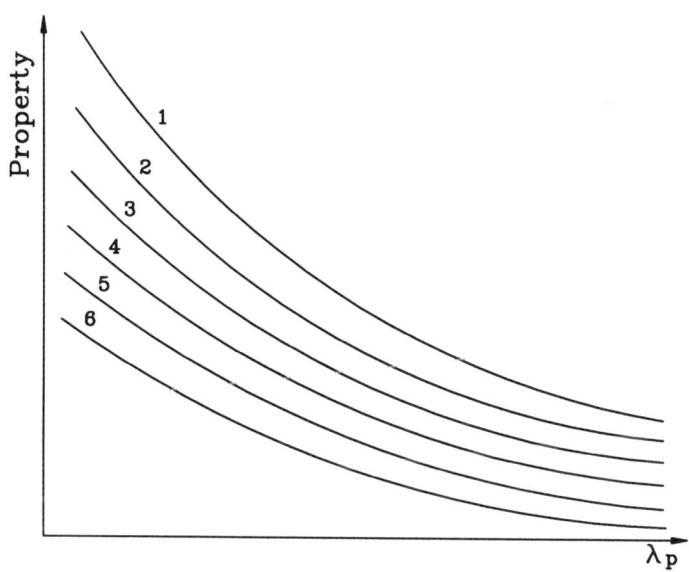

Figure 4.1. Variation of behavior with sphericity.

1. Self-orientedness or Selfishness

Self-orientedness is an orientation towards the self (selfishness). The degree of selfishness in the individual is the degree of preoccupation with the self in the individual's thoughts, motives, actions and behavior. An extremely selfish individual is exclusively concerned about himself and his own interests always.

Selfishness prompts an individual to think and act to protect or promote his own interests at the expense of others. It is part of a general self-defense strategy, which, as we have seen, originates from a feeling of insecurity, a feeling that one is vulnerable to forces outside of oneself.

While every human being is selfish (since everyone is imperfect and feels insecure; no one has a λ_p of 1.00), the degree of selfishness varies from one individual to the other. Hence you will hear people making such comments as, "That man is very selfish."

Since it results directly from insecurity, selfishness will be highest at low λ_p and lowest at high λ_p. When λ_p is low, the individual moves to protect his fragile self by concentrating his thoughts and actions on himself almost exclusively, and by always monitoring himself with respect to his environment. A person whose sphericity is high on the other hand does not feel that much insecurity and hence is more 'natural' (unguarded) and can afford to be more selfless than the former.

While we are all selfish to one degree or another, it is very hard for us to acknowledge that. We like to think of ourselves as gentle doves who are so selfless that everyone around us is taking advantage of us. So in order to identify where selfishness exists and to what degree it exists there we may have to rely on other characteristics of the individual that point to his insecurity.

2. Not Considerate Of Other People

Lower λ_p individuals (selfish) are usually not considerate of other people in their drive to protect their own interests and get their own share out of life. In other words, they think of themselves only first and later (if at all) consider others when their needs have been met. As sphericity increases and the intensity of insecurity decreases people become more and more considerate of others until at very high sphericities you

Need for Self-defense 43

can find individuals willing to give their lives for others, expecting nothing in return.

The lower sphericity individual is always "looking out for number one" while the high sphericity person on the other end is "looking out for all of us." Everyone is altruistic once in a while but the low sphericity individual gives to satisfy his need to be greater than others (to be discussed later), to show the world and himself that he is a good man, to get praise or as part of a general strategy. The very high sphericity individual gives because it is the right thing to do, expecting to get no other reward from it.

No wonder the low sphericity person is much wiser and smarter than the high sphericity individual in the everyday stuff of life.

The more selfish individual is more apt to feel that he is doing too much or giving too much to others because every excursion outside of himself is a "great" event. The high sphericity (less selfish) individual, on the other hand, even when he does something great for the other person, is more inclined to insist (and feel down deep in himself, we suppose) that he has not done anything extraordinary—'it was just the right thing to do.' It is more natural for him to consider others than it is for the lower λ_p individual.

Another point to note is that because of the inability of low sphericity individuals to see from other viewpoints (that is why they are not considerate of others), they often feel little or no guilt even when they commit heinous crimes against another. They have a special knack for justifying everything in their favor. They are therefore less likely to accept blame for anything they do or say. The high sphericity individual on the other hand, feels guilty when he does something bad and accepts blame more readily because he can consider other view points more.

Further, because of their higher dose of insecurity, lower λ_p persons don't like to hear that they did anything wrong. In other words, they are touchy, very touchy, about criticism. Too weak or too insecure to look at the other side. Higher λ_p individuals can take constructive criticisms, without feeling uneasy or slighted. They are better at factoring in other people's views without losing theirs.

Unable or too insecure to see from the other side, lower λ_p persons tend to be vengeful, unforgiving, and vindictive. Because of their innate ability to see from the other person's angle and consider his weakness, higher λ_p persons are usually very forgiving, to the point where they may be considered "weak."

3. Need To Be On Guard

Insecurity breeds the need to be on guard. Extremely insecure individuals have a tremendous need to be on guard, because of the unconsciously perceived weakness discussed above. They think that everyone is out to get them or their properties. Every individual has an element of this characteristic, its intensity decreasing as you go from the low sphericity end to the high sphericity end.

A person with a high need to be on guard (low λ_p) is very suspicious of others and his environment. They (low λ_p individuals) are very vulnerable to fears and suspicions about other groups, races, religions, etc. Their group, race, religion, region, etc. is either the best or the one and only. So, they are usually very susceptible to racism and all forms of hate.

Consumed with mistrust and suspicion, they are exceptionally aware of their environment. When they enter a house, for example, they are immediately aware of what is where and what is not where. They seem to be always scanning situations and people around them for possible danger signals. They are exceptionally good at picking up mixed messages, subtlety, body language and hidden motivations. Sometimes they fall victim to misinterpreting the "hidden intentions" they perceive. Not everyone has an underhanded motivation.

A person of high sphericity does not feel the same intensity of insecurity as a low sphericity individual so he never develops this need to be on guard very well. Lacking this defense mechanism, their natural dispositions flow out more freely, without the usual trying to remain on guard and protect oneself so prevalent in the rest of us. This free-flowing behavior is probably what Maslow (1976) refers to as "the free radioactive expression of the deep person." (p.54). Such individuals are usually very honest, trusting and naive, often unaware of the deviousness and underhanded motives of the people they deal with—resulting in more experiences of disappointments, failures and mistreatments in their relationships than most people.

In addition to being defensive and guarded, people with a great need to be on guard are also secretive; always hiding one thing or the other from all those dangerous souls out there. Their guard duties may make them appear independent and introverted but they are not: they keep their distances from others for self-defense purposes.

4. Cunningness and Tactfulness

It follows from the above that the more selfish an individual is, the smarter he is. He almost always expects to be exploited or harmed by others, so he is always on guard. Being always alert, it is hard for a situation to overtake him that he wouldn't know how to pull himself out. Low λ_p individuals are very cunning, treacherous, maneuvering, indirect, shrewd and tactful in their dealings with other people—all in a bid to protect oneself.

The higher sphericity individual is not so endowed and must depend on other means to promote his survival in the jungle of life. You would find the high sphericity individual so tactless, honest and extraordinarily direct in his dealings that you'll wonder whether he has any brains at all. Because high sphericity individuals are too trusting, it is practically very easy for them to be taken to the cleaners. (Low λ_p persons with a high need to avoid reality are also easy prey for con artists).

5. Deliberate Faking

The more insecure (i.e. the lower the sphericity) an individual is, the greater the need to fake things or lie in order to protect one's weakness (a part of a general self-defense strategy). Deliberate faking goes hand-in-hand with the ability to speak and act to blend in with the situation. Fakers are usually not consistent and change their colors with changes in their surroundings. People who score high on this trait are usually very smart in other areas of their lives too.

High sphericity individuals do not feel that much need to protect themselves so they are not good at faking or blending in with the situation. They are usually solidly consistent. Research psychologists or market analysts can depend on their self-reports.

6. Practical, Present-oriented

Self-centered individuals (low sphericity) are usually very practical, again because of the perceived insecurity discussed before. They are not interested in high-flying theories or schemes that have no relevance to their present needs. "What is in it for me?" is their constant cry. They are completely oriented to the present, not the future.

It follows then that they like to stay with what is certain, proven, concrete, familiar, and established. They don't want to expose themselves to unknown forces. They are not interested in things that are abstract, experimental, tentative, iffy, speculative, or strange. High sphericity individuals, on the other hand, are at

Need for Self-defense 47

home with the theoretical and imaginative side of life—they do not feel the same intensity of insecurity that causes lower sphericity individuals to hang on to the tried, tested and true. Because of their ability to stay with the fluid (not concrete) side of life, they are more able to chase down elusive thoughts and ideas and make them serve the needs of man.

Summary

Low λp	High λp
1. More self-oriented or selfish	1. More us-oriented and selfless
2. Concentrates thoughts and actions on self	2. Concentrates thoughts and actions more on all of us
3. Less considerate of other people	3. More considerate of other people
4. Feels he is giving too much	4. Feels it's just the right thing to do
5. Feels little or no guilt	5. Feels guilty when wrong
6. Unlikely to accept blame	6. More likely to accept blame
7. Vengeful, unforgiving, vindictive	7. More forgiving
9. Very touchy about criticism	9. Can live with constructive criticism
10. More need to be on guard, secretive	10. Less need to be on guard, open
11. Very susceptible to prejudice and hate	11. Less susceptible to prejudice and hate

12. Excellent at picking up subtlety and hidden motivations	12. Less able to pick up subtlety and hidden motivations
13. Cunning and tactful	13. Direct and tactless
14. Smart	14. Naive
15. Deliberate faking	15. Inability to disguise
16. Lie "honestly"	16. Scrupulously honest
17. Blend in seamlessly	17. Less able to blend in
18. Practical, present-oriented	18. Theoretical, future-oriented
19. What is in it for me?	19. What may be in it for us?
20. Hang on to the tried, tested and true	20. At home with the fluid side of life

NOTE:

As we will see when we discuss φ_p, competition affects how secure an individual feels. A highly competitive society makes people more insecure than less competitive societies. This means that the traits associated with selfishness or the need for self-defense will be more pronounced in competitive societies than in non-competitive societies.

Further, if a person's φ_p is such that he depends on or is supposed to depend on someone else to take care of him, the need for self-defense may not be fully emphasized in his behavior. Similarly, a high φ_p individual is socially secure and may not stress self-defense behavior fully. When conditions or attitudes change, this need may gain more intensity. In order to understand a person's true biological behavior, λ_p, it is therefore necessary to consider φ_p. Don't worry if you can't see at the moment how the comments in this note relate to our discussion. You will figure it out when we discuss φ_p later.

Chapter Five

Breadth Of View

The breadth of view trait dimension has already been touched on when we examined the need for self-defense—under being considerate of others. You will notice this sort of overlap throughout our discussions because we are discussing characteristics springing from one single source: insecurity or lack of it.

This trait dimension has received lots of attention in the literature, especially in the areas of divergent thinking and creativity. We shall discuss it here by referring to the two ends of the continuum—narrow-view and broadview.

People characterized as low sphericity in this model has narrow view while those with high sphericity has broadview. As selfishness decreases from low to high sphericity, the breadth of view increases. Low λ_p persons have narrow-view compasses that is why they are selfish and not very considerate of others. High sphericity (more secure) individuals on the other hand are less selfish because they have broader views that incorporate others in their instinctive decision making and cognitive processes.

Think of a broadview individual as someone who takes an aerial view of the whole city and sees the point where he is standing in reference to other points in his picture. Imagine the narrow-view individual as someone who takes a picture of the place where he is and from that understands his immediate surroundings but has no idea (and probably doesn't want to know) how the place he is standing and his immediate surroundings relate to the whole city.

The narrow-view/broadview characteristic goes beyond selfishness or lack thereof in day to day activities. It affects an individual's orientation to life and his natural abilities. Here are some behavioral characteristics that indicate broadview in an individual:

1. Keen awareness of self and abilities
2. Eager to serve the human race
3. Curious and open to experience
4. Likely to search for needed information from a wide range of sources
5. Uneasy with the status quo
6. Tolerant of ambiguity
7. Ability to view problems in multiple perspectives
8. Able to spot broadview problems, like problems in an academic discipline
9. Exceptionally good at global planning but not very good at local planning
10. Has more ideas on a subject than others
11. Able to see overriding patterns, order, system, or structure in the flux of experience or data

12. Ability to form 'remote' associations between concepts in different domains
13. A future orientation in relative and contextual terms
14. Critical of falsehoods and pretenders

The general variations of the above characteristics with λ_p are shown in Figure 5.1.

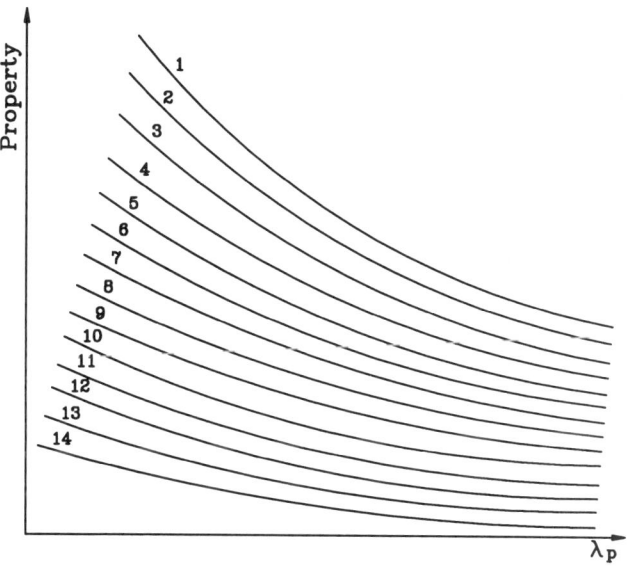

Figure 5.1. Variation of behavior with sphericity.

1. Keen Awareness of Self and Abilities

A broadview individual (especially at very high sphericity levels) instinctively knows who is, what he wants to achieve and his own place in the scheme of things (owing to his unconscious 'aerial view' discussed above). Depending on the level of education or exposure, he can reasonably determine what his destiny is.

As λ_p decreases, individuals begin to have difficulties connecting with their deep self. They therefore need guidance in finding who they are and their place in the world.

2. Eager to Serve the Human Race

Since broadview individuals (high λ_p) see something like an aerial picture of the world, they tend to see themselves as part of other human beings in the world. They tend to think that to achieve happiness everyone should serve the needs of everyone, so they tend to be largely concerned with the welfare of others. The broadview individual is always pursuing a greater good. The narrow view individual, on the other hand, does not see others in that light in his world view. All he sees is a world where everyone is out for himself. "It's a jungle out there, you either kill or be killed." The lower λ_p person is therefore wiser than the high λ_p individuals in the affairs of life.

3. Curious and Open to Experience

Because they can see wider and understand that there are lots more to see than what is immediately available to them, high λ_p individuals have stronger desires to know more about the world around them than low λ_p persons. Here we are talking about knowledge beyond that required for self-defense.

Curiosity leads them to abhor the overly familiar. They love to see more than they are seeing now, to ask questions that have not been asked, to find out more than what is already known. They have a remarkable ability to be surprised, to be puzzled and to regard new information with curiosity, with little or no censorship. They tend to get bored easily once they have mastered a particular job or field. Breadth seems to be more important to them than depth. They love to toy with ideas. Lower λ_p individuals, on the other hand, love to hone their skills and dig deeper into the fields they are already involved in.

There is no need for them to deny or distort any experience to defend their weakness as the case with lower sphericity individuals, so broadview persons are able to remain fully open to experience.

4. Likely to Search for Needed Information From a Wide Range of Sources

Being curious and open, the broadview individual will tend to read extensively in a broad range of materials. He will typically have interest in many fields and may be eclectic in his research efforts if he is in academics. Lower λ_p individuals stay with materials already identified to be related to their work.

5. Uneasy With the Status Quo

Broadview capability disposes high λ_p individuals to see more of the whole picture so they are usually uneasy with the status quo which is almost always settled into one corner or the other of the total picture. Their readiness to stand back and question assumptions and beliefs, to take a detached point of view to see the data or problem in larger, broader perspectives puts them out of step with the status quo. Narrow-view individuals are usually satisfied with the status quo, unless their own share is in jeopardy.

6. Tolerant of Ambiguity

Broadview individuals have high tolerances for ambiguity because of their instinctive ability to consider the whole picture. They can live for a while with conflicting ideas. More insecure people (lower λ_p) find uncertainty and ambiguity too heavy or stressful to bear. Higher λ_p individuals tend to treat the unknown or the unusual as a challenge rather than as a threat to be avoided. Lower λ_p individuals prefer to stay with the tried, tested and true. They find unusual circumstances or uncertainties threatening and flee from them as soon as they can.

Broadview persons are also able to empathize with ideas that diverge from their own, and thus they are capable of combining their existing ideas with those that are new to them.

7. Ability to View Problems in Multiple Perspectives

The broad view capability gives high sphericity individuals a greater ability to view problems in multiple perspectives—from an abstract perspective to a down-to-earth viewpoint. Lower λ_p persons have a hard time seeing beyond what they already know or risking a different point of view. Insecurity chains them to a narrow-view perspective.

8. Able to Spot Broadview Problems, Like Problems in an Academic Discipline

High sphericity individuals have a special knack for spotting broadview problems before anyone else. Due to their broader explorations they seem to be able to hit directly at the soul of the problem. It must be pointed out that they are not good at spotting narrow view problems like being dealt an underhand in day to day matters. As λ_p decreases the ability to spot broadview problems decreases.

9. Exceptionally Good at Global Planning But Not Very Good at Local Planning

High sphericity individuals are exceptionally good at global (overall) planning because of their unconscious broadview capability but they are usually not good at local planning. Let them develop a general strategy or a general theory but get others to fill in the details and complete the picture. In academics, broadview individuals are better at coming up with simple, compact, comprehensive theories but they are usually not very good at filling in the on-the-ground details of a picture that has already been created. The narrower view individuals are great at routine science but not very good at coming up with parsimonious, generalized theories.

10. Has More Ideas on a Subject Than Others

Since they can naturally scan a broader information base than most others, high sphericity individuals usually come up with more ideas when ideas are wanted on a particular subject, especially if it is their subject of interest—and their ideas tend to be good. This ability decreases as λ_p decreases.

11. Able to See Overriding Patterns, Order, System, or Structure in the Flux Of Experience or Data

High sphericity individuals are much more able to discover overriding patterns, order, system, or structure in a mass of data or in the flux of experience. For one thing their natural tendency towards broadview means that they are more concerned about order and structure than the rest of us. Lower λ_p persons are more concerned about protecting their own turf and polishing their corner than about order and structure.

12. Ability to Form 'Remote' Associations Between Concepts in Different Domains

High sphericity individuals have another special ability most of us don't have as much: the innate ability to form 'remote' associations between concepts in different domains. Scanning broadly as nature seem to incline them to do they are able to spot associations between concepts in different domains which does not immediately appear to us to be connected. At first sight, these connections seem to be "divinely" or supernaturally aided but they are not. There is nothing divine, supernatural or extraordinary about connections in fields we tend to see as unconnected. All of nature is one whole and the broadview persons among us see more of this whole than the rest of us.

Because of this natural ability, high sphericity individuals tend to reason by analogies, similes and metaphors, more often than the rest of us.

13. A Future Orientation in Relative and Contextual Terms

Closely related to their broadview in ideas, high sphericity individuals have a future orientation. They are able to spot a broad outline that could lead to something in the future and they are willing to go through pain in the present in order to reap benefits or see their ideas succeed in the future. Their strong belief in themselves (self-confidence and self-sufficiency) coupled with their native hopeful outlook (high sphericity individuals tend to be eternal optimists because they can see broadly) serve them well here. We all have this future orientation but high sphericity individuals score highest on this trait.

14. Critical of Falsehoods and Pretenders

Since broadview individuals can see more of the total picture than most people, they tend to be able to spot flaws, falsehoods and general pretensions better than the rest of us. Because they can put most things in their proper perspective, they tend to be critical and look with disdain or disapproval on us when we are pretending and glorying in our little corner that we are the entire universe.

Summary

Low λ_p	High λ_p
1. Difficulty connecting with his/her place in the world	1. Keen awareness of self and place in the world
2. Eager to fulfil selfish interests	2. Eager to serve the human race
3. Sticks to what is already known	3. Curious and very open to experience
4. Dig deeper into related materials	4. Search for information from a wide range of sources
5. Satisfied with the status quo	5. Uneasy with the status quo
6. Flee from uncertainty and ambiguity	6. Tolerant of uncertainty and ambiguity
7. Hard time seeing problems in many perspectives	7. Ability to view problems in multiple perspectives
8. Not good at spotting broadview problems	8. Very good at spotting broadview problems
9. Good at local planning, poor at global planning	9. Good at global planning, poor at local planning
10. Has few good original ideas on a subject	10. Has many good ideas on a subject
11. Not good at seeing overall order and structure	11. Very good at seeing overall order and structure
12. Find it hard to see remote associations	12. Able to see remote associations
13. An orientation to the present	13. An orientation towards the future
14. See pretenders as normal and smart	14. Very critical of falsehoods and pretenders

NOTE:

A low φ_p deflates a person's self-confidence and makes him fixate more on his immediate survival so that his broadview capability may not show but when he gains more empowerment (i.e. his φ_p increases) his natural breadth of view will shine through. So φ_p must be taken into consideration in the study of λ_p. Later chapters discuss φ_p further.

Chapter Six

Need to Avoid Reality

Reality is often a difficult subject to face because many times it is different from what we want it to be. Difficulties with reality arise because of:

- our inability to control the actions of others and the events unfolding around us,
- the fear and risk involved in not knowing what is going to happen next,
- the unending uncertainties we are condemned to experience every day,
- the unexpected circumstances that often trip our well-made plans,
- the obstacles we must overcome to get to our goals,
- the tough decisions that we must make,

- the risk of being wrong,
- the secret fear that we may not be able to cope, etc.

So we all, in varying degrees, try to cope with the stress of living by trying to escape from, avoid or ignore reality. We shall discuss the several ways we do this under the following topics:

1. Flee or dodge reality
2. Fantasy
3. Daredevil adventures, gambling
4. Vanity
5. Alcoholism and drug abuse
6. Gossip

These characteristics vary with λp as shown in Figure 6.1.

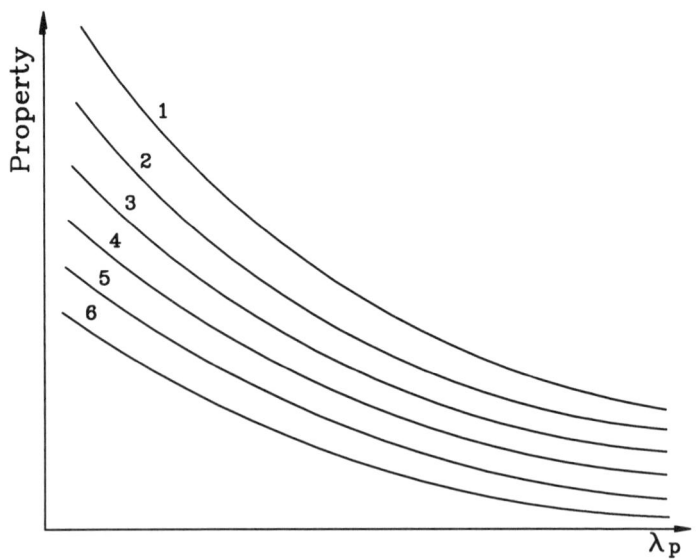

Figure 6.1. Variation of behavior with sphericity.

Need to Avoid Reality 61

1. Flee Or Dodge Reality

Our insecurities and disappointing experiences in life make us feel inadequate to confront reality—reality feels heavy to us. We feel helpless in the face of hostile reality and/or our responsibilities. We complain, we swear, we regret our existence, we procrastinate, we try to flee from them. We wish we could find a strong person to take care of us and protect us from the ugly sides of reality—someone to take over and face reality for us—but it never happens to our satisfaction. Sometimes we find someone willing and able to shoulder our burdens for us but in the course of facing reality for us he also takes away our freedom, our throbbing heartbeat and our right to be human. So we decide to live our lives ourselves.

We try to distance ourselves from our duties but no matter how long we put off our responsibilities they have an uncanny ability to stick to us. We also try (or fantasize) to be someone else—a celebrity, anyone we think is not subject to the same kind of onslaught of reality as we are.

We all share in this feeling of helplessness or discomfort with reality but it is stronger in some of us than in others. The lower the sphericity (our measure of insecurity), the stronger the intensity of the feeling of helplessness, consciously or unconsciously (φ_p being equal). Lower λ_p persons tend to flee or seek shelter from reality more frequently and more intensely than high λ_p individuals. In other words, the general survival plan of very insecure people emphasizes avoidance of reality more than that of more secure people (φ_p being equal).

You will find people who score high on the need to avoid reality often seeking help from experts, gurus, psychics, fortune-tellers, anyone who can help them escape the harsh edges of reality.

2. Fantasy

Fantasy is one of the highly useful defense mechanisms the human mind invented to help us take our eyes off reality, at least for a while. We fantasize about everything, from a brave new world where righteousness reigns to a love ferry sweeping us off our feet and taking us to a peaceful land of romantic bliss. How sweet it is to dwell in that angelic land of endless glee!

Our fiction writers and producers have honed and aimed their skills to locate this string in the electrical room of our being and switch it on with book after book, and movie after movie, of sensational fantasy. And we are grateful for them. It is always refreshing to take a break once in a while from the battery of reality and walk on the beautiful, care-free shores of the imaginary. It becomes a problem however when we decide to abandon reality altogether and bask and bathe in the never-ending sunshine of vanity land. Our contract with life requires that we breathe our own air and face the consequences of being alive. Any time we infringe on this contract, life has a way of exacting an appropriate recompense.

The need to fantasize and imagine better worlds than what reality allows varies from high in low sphericity individuals to low in high sphericity individuals. Low sphericity individuals try to cope with stress by ignoring reality more than high sphericity persons.

3. Daredevil Adventures; Gambling

Another form of ignoring reality is taking more than a healthy dose of chances—daredevil adventures and gambling. As human beings with a need for fantasy, we sometimes engage in reckless, high-risk (chance) activities and gambling. The peak experience (the thrill, the sensation) that results from these adventures help calm our deep feelings of inadequacy and insecurity. It lets us know that we are alive, significant and powerful and not as inadequate as our weak inner-core keeps telling us. It feels good to know that once in a while we can deliberately thumb our noses at "reality" and win. Notice that gambling is a form of adventure—it involves beating the odds like every other form of thrill-seeking adventure.

When a high need for self-defense does not cover it, the need for daredevil adventures and thrill is higher at low λ_p than at high λ_p. Adventurous individuals will go out of their ways to seek thrill and enjoy it. Higher sphericity persons may not seek adventurous situations but if they have to pass through it, they would.

4. Vanity

A concentration on vain things that add little or nothing to the task of handling reality is another way we try to distract ourselves from reality. Paying too much attention to grooming, style, and fashion, and all those "fine" things in life, is nothing but vanity and a distraction from the real business of living. But they are good distractions—helping us to fulfil our need for vanity and providing us with a chance to try a different pace in our lives.

High sphericity individuals tend to disdain vanity while low sphericity persons adore and crave it but all of us indulge in a degree of vanity once in a while. The greater the degree of vanity in a person's life, the higher the need to avoid reality. Please note that some people do not emphasis vanity in their lives because they don't have the means to do so.

5. Alcoholism And Drug Abuse

Alcoholism and drug abuse are other ways some of us try to live in the world without having to face reality. These substances help transport us out of the realm of reality for a while and then bring us home when the fuel is used up. Once we experience the thrill of taking refuge from reality in these ways we seek to multiply it, thereby reducing our ability to deal with life and fulfil our lives in the real world.

Again, the tendency to do this is higher among lower sphericity individuals than higher sphericity persons (φ_p being equal), unless where it is hindered by a high need for self-defense which usually emphasizes caution. Alcoholism and drug abuse will be high among adventurous individuals.

6. Gossip

We often prefer gossip to the weighty matters of existence. Reality is tough, exacting and direct. We prefer to avoid it by resorting to discussing other people, their weak points and their failures. It helps us to ignore the reality of our own existence and imperfections while it lasts. Everybody likes to gossip, the intensity and frequency with which we resort to it being lower at high sphericity than at low sphericity.

Summary

Low λ_p	High λ_p
1. More likely to flee difficult challenges	1. Less likely to flee difficult challenges
2. High need for fantasy	2. Little need for fantasy
3. More likely to take daredevil chances and gamble	3. Less likely to take daredevil chances and gamble
4. Crave and adore vanity	4. Disdain vanity
5. More susceptible to alcoholism and drug abuse	5. Less susceptible to alcoholism and drug abuse
6. More likely to prefer gossip to weighty matters	6. Less likely to prefer gossip to weighty matters

Chapter Seven

Need for Others

Man is by nature a social animal; an individual who is unsocial naturally and not accidently is either beneath our notice or more than human.
   Society is something in nature that precedes the individual. Anyone who either cannot lead the common life or is so self-sufficient as not to need to, and therefore does not partake of society, is either a beast or a god

Aristotle
Politics, c. 328 B.C.

The need for others is one other need that results from our insecurity. At first sight it looks as if it is not driven by insecurity but it is. One reason for this is that we were born helpless, inadequate to handle all the issues of our own existence. At birth we needed other people to help us survive, we simply couldn't do it on our own. With time we begin to develop strengths and resources of our own and the need for others to help us at every turn decreases but it never fully goes away.

We are social animals because our insecurities invite us to seek the company of one another. It is our feelings of inadequacy and vulnerability in the world that make us live in groups and seek to associate with one another. This need is so great that nothing else can be compared to it. We depend on others, on society, for so much in our lives that our social life is almost as important as our personal life.

Aronson's Gain-Loss theory (Aronson 1984, p.307-314) and the experimental results that validate it clearly demonstrate that the feeling of love, for example, is driven by insecurity. It is not innate in us as our blood or bones for example. The theory suggests that increases in a positive, rewarding behavior from another person have more impact on an individual than constant, invariant reward from that person. In other words, if you love someone sweetly all the time, no matter what he does, that person will not feel your love as he will feel the love of someone whose intensity of love for him varies—sometimes he loves him, sometimes he doesn't. The insecurity (resulting from the potential difference) created by the variability makes the love sweeter.

The need for others is driven by and sustained by insecurity. Put another way, we need other people to help us deal with reality which we realize is beyond our absolute control.

Since the need for others is driven by insecurity, it will follow the same trend as the need for self-defense. The greater the insecurity, the greater the need for the love and appreciation of others. This means that low λ_p individuals have a greater need for others than high λ_p persons. To examine this trait

further, we shall look at the following sub-levels of its manifestation:
1. Group-orientedness
2. Need for compliments and praise
3. Need to be center of attention
4. Life of the party
5. Love to connect and build a network of friends
6. Response to social processing
7. Response to external control
8. Social skills
9. Need for help
10. Sex and romance

The general variations of the above characteristics with λ_p is given in Figure 7.1.

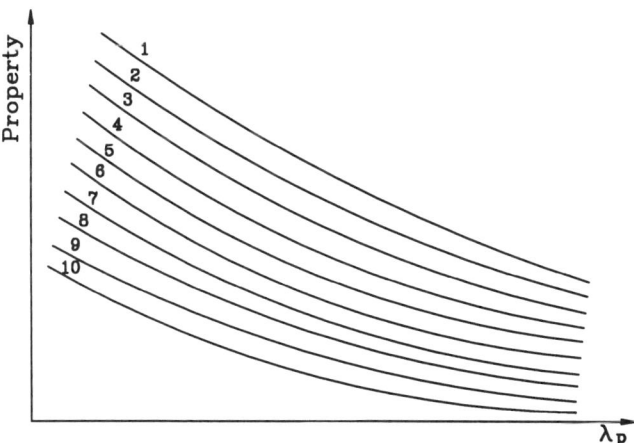

Figure 7.1. Variation of behavior with sphericity.

1. Group-orientedness

Human beings tend to like and to do things that meet one or the other of their natural needs, whether they realize it or not. Any activity that does not support, or at least tend to support, one human need or the other cannot succeed in the world of men and women.

It is obvious that those who are group-oriented have a need for others and those who are not group-oriented do not need others as much. Everybody needs other people but the intensity of the need for others varies from one individual to another, being greater in some people than in others.

In this model, we define the need for others as the extraversion-introversion continuum. The greater the need for others, the greater the degree of extraversion and the lower the degree of introversion. The lower the need for others the lower the degree of extraversion and the greater the degree of introversion.

From our discussions above, it is apparent that lower sphericity individuals feel (unconsciously) greater inadequacy and insecurity than higher sphericity individuals. They therefore naturally need others as part of their equipment in the game of survival and self-fulfillment more than high λ_p persons. The need for others (extraversion, in this model) will therefore be greater as the sphericity decreases and lower as it increases. Extraverts are more group-oriented than introverts.

High sphericity individuals, on the other hand, feel less inadequate or insecure and are therefore less inclined toward group activities. While they may make group happiness their major concern, they usually don't need other people as part of their survival or pursuit-of-happiness package. They are OK on their own. In other words they are more self-sufficient but never totally without the need for others.

Extraverts have burning desires to connect with others, to be with other people, while introverts are self-sufficient and prefer to spend time alone doing their own thing. Being alone feels very heavy to extraverts but extreme introverts crave solitude, they wouldn't feel that anything is missing from their

Need for Others 69

lives if they are alone. Because of this lack of enthusiasm for group activities, it seems to this author that most introverts will be incompetent at such group activities like sports.

The desire to be alone will also be prevalent at very low sphericities as suspicion of others and the need to be on guard drive otherwise natural extraverts to wall themselves up against the "dangerous world" out there. If the world was not such a dangerous and slippery slope for these individuals, they would love to connect with others and their natural smartness would make them very good at group games. You may mistake their loneliness for high sphericity if you don't know any better. The best way, we would suggest, to distinguish between very insecure people who appear self-sufficient because they withdraw from others for self-defense purposes and high λ_p persons is by their vindictiveness. As we saw earlier, very low λ_p individuals tend to be wicked, cruel and vindictive while high sphericity persons tend to be kind and very forgiving. Many traits associated with high sphericity in the need for others or self-sufficiency will appear to be present in very low sphericity persons who avoid or distance themselves from people for security purposes. You will know them by the fact that they score high in other dimensions associated with high insecurity.

The need for others is a very powerful force in human affairs and human beings can easily be categorized on its basis. The Myers-Briggs data presented by Tieger and Barron-Tieger (1995) show the following breakdown in characteristic preferences:

Extraversion	72%	Introversion	28%
Sensing	76%	Intuition	24%
Thinking	50%	Feeling	50%
Judging	50%	Perceiving	50%

This appears to suggest that Thinking-Feeling and Judging-Perceiving in the Myers-Briggs personality inventory are irrelevant as distinguishing characteristics. The numbers above show that the Myers-Briggs personality typing divides people into two groups: sensing extraverts and intuitive introverts. About seventy-five per cent (75%) of the people are extraverts and about twenty-five per cent (25%) are introverts.

The implication of this is that most of us are more likely to find our happiness in the domain of relationships than anywhere else. It never ceases to amaze this author how little we invest into this all-important aspect of our lives. We take tremendous risks and put in lots of thought, time, money and effort into our work but pay very little attention to our relationships. Yet for our happiness (at least for the vast majority of us) our relationships are more important than any other one thing.

2. Need for Compliments and Praise

One of the deepest cravings of the human mind is the desire to be appreciated and praised. It comes from our insecurity. We need the approval of others to tell our fragile, insecure selves that we are on the right course. As expected, this need or desire varies from individual to individual. Low λ_p persons need compliments and praise as a fish needs water to survive. High sphericity individuals, on the other hand, will not suffer in their absence because their craving for them are not that high (owing to the fact that they feel more secure in their personal worlds).

3. Need to Be the Center of Attention

Extraverts love to be seen, heard or appreciated. They thirst for attention, soaking it up wherever they spot it. Some seek to be center of attention in the larger society, others seek the same thing in smaller groups or families. The higher the extraversion score, the greater the need to be the center of attention. The social image of extraverts is so very important to them, as it should be since they need approval badly. How will people react to me if I wear this, say this, do this, etc.?

For the high sphericity individuals, on the other end, social image is not very important. Because they don't instinctively need people, they pay little or no attention to what people think about them. You can think or say anything you want about them and they simply won't mind. They have a natural inclination to avoid being the center of attention. Mature introverts learn however, very reluctantly, to present themselves in a favorable social light. Nobody needs to be told that in a largely social world one needs to be socially accessible. If you don't look or act your social part you are going no where fast, at least not in a world dominated by extraverts like ours.

4. Life of the Party

Extraverts (low λ_p persons) love to get together with others to have fun and explore other aspects of their lives. They enjoy parties and social gatherings. Introverts, on the other hand, feel out of their elements at parties and social get-togethers. The extraverts end up having a good time and the introverts end up whining about the precious time they "wasted" at the party.

5. Love to Connect and Build a Network of Friends

Extraverts love to go out and meet people and make more friends. The more people they can count as friends the happier they are. Like every other characteristic, some extraverts prefer to do this more than others. Introverts have difficulty or little desire to connect with others. Connecting with people and making friends feel heavy to them while they energize and brighten the life of extraverts.

6. Response to Social Processing

Extraverts respond more to social processing than introverts. Their need for others and other characteristics that come with their relatively lower sphericities make extraverts conform better to social standards than introverts. Some extraverts may decide to be different from society at large but conform readily to their "own" groups.

Extreme introverts hardly conform to any group standard without questioning it to determine if it agrees with their highly-priced internal (personal) values. While they may be dedicated to the causes of groups they are connected to, they maintain their own set of principles, some of which may not agree with the group. They are fiercely self-sufficient, independent and nonconformist (please note that extraverts can also choose not to conform but to introverts it comes more naturally). Introverts are usually the kind of students who passed through the school but the school did not pass through them. Rigidly self-sufficient and independent, they hardly pick up the lifestyle and value system of the social processing unit. They come out almost as they went in.

History tends to support the idea that most of mankind's great advances have been made by nonconformists—those who are unafraid to be different, to deviate from the general course. Bernard Shaw is quoted to have said that "the reasonable (i.e the sociable, conforming individual) adapts himself to the world, the unreasonable one (the high λ_p person in our model) persists in trying to adapt the world to himself. Therefore all progress depends upon the unreasonable man."

Nonconforming individuals tend to be "strongly motivated to achieve in situations in which independence of thought and action is called for and... have much less interest or motivation to achieve in situations which demand conforming behavior" (MacKinnon, 1965, p.164).

But nonconformism is not as desirable as you might imagine. "Nonconformists," Aronson wrote, "may be praised by historians or idolized in films or literature long after the fact of their nonconformity, but they are usually not held in high esteem, at the time, by those people to whose demands they refuse to conform" (Aronson, 1984, p.15). In real life nonconformism brings a lot of pain and suffering to nonconformists.

7. Response to External Control

Introverts are "sufficient unto themselves" and vehemently reject policing and external control. They don't follow administrative rules well and they hate to be told what to do. But unlike extraverted radicals who love to appear as introverts, introverts are very good workers, displaying tremendous drive and thoroughness in their work. They just don't want you putting them in strait jackets. Extraverts have no such strong aversion to regulation.

8. Social Skills

Introverts are naturally less socially skilled and less "well-rounded" than extraverts. Because they don't really see the need to connect with others, they unconsciously, we believe, fail to muster enough enthusiasm to learn and hone social skills. Needless to say, if they intend to live in this world they will suffer many deprivations or deficiencies because of this. We live in societies and social skills are very important whether you like it or not.

9. Need for Help

Introverts seldom ask for help. They are self-sufficient. As graduate students, for instance, they usually don't ask for help from their colleagues or professors. Imagine being the academic supervisor of one of them. How does it feel to be almost totally ignored, seemingly unneeded and removed from the work of your student? Most introverts will understand their fellow introverts but most of us (the extraverts) will feel slighted and mad!

10. Need for Sex and Romance

While extraverts relish sex and romance, introverts are often self-sufficient even when it comes to sex. They are usually, relatively speaking, low on sexual needs. Extreme introverts won't suffer in the absence of sex. Extraverts are naturally romantically active and vibrant while introverts are boring and romantically flat.

11. Self-sufficiency Looks Like Arrogance

The self-sufficiency trait in introverts may make them appear arrogant but in most cases introverts are humble. Their natural broadview capability make them realize their place in the scheme of things and they are usually humble. But being ruggedly independent and self-sufficient, plus their natural disposition toward broadview characteristics, they are bound to be mistaken for proud people.

Need for Others

Summary

Low λ_p	High λ_p
1. Group-oriented	1. Little need for others
2. Great need to be appreciated and praised	2. Little need for appreciation and praise
3. Need to be center of attention	3. Avoids being the center of attention
4. Life of the party	4. Not interested in parties
5. Love to connect with others and make friends	5. Have difficulty or little desire to connect with others
6. Conforms readily to social standards	6. Does not conform readily to social standards
7. No strong aversion to regulation	7. Rejects policing and external control
8. More socially skilled and well-rounded	8. Less socially skilled and well-rounded
9. Ask for help	9. Seldom ask for help
10. Relish sex and romance	10. Low on sex and romance

NOTE:

If someone's position in society is determined by whether the person is loved, cherished and appreciated (i.e. the person's φ_p is so low that he has to depend on someone else for survival or the society requires that the person be loved in order for him to gain status), the person may be forced to lose himself (become or fake being "selfless," undemanding, loyal, non-competitive, humble, nice—making him behave like someone with a very high λ_p) so that others may love him, because it is easier to win love and protection that way. His apparent need for others will therefore be high, much higher than his λ_p alone would have produced. But when or if that societal position changes or his φ_p increases, the person's true nature will burst into the open. For this reason, we stress in this book that in order to understand a person's true λ_p, his φ_p should be considered. φ_p is discussed more in later chapters.

Chapter Eight

Need to Be Greater than Others

The need to be greater than others is closely related to the need to be in control (part of the self-defense package already discussed). This need arises from a sense of insecurity occasioned by our inadequacy. If we can show that we are better or greater than others it helps us to vindicate ourselves, to calm our deep feelings of inadequacy and insecurity. At low sphericities, the need to be greater than others and/or the need to be in control of others is very high and it decreases as the sphericity increases.

The desire to be greater than others is driven by the notion that if I am greater than the next person I must in some way be controlling the reality of my existence well enough to be greater than someone—an assurance that I am strong despite the wrenching feeling of insecurity deep down in my stomach that I am inadequate. Without this feeling of insecurity, the need to be greater than others will not arise in the first place. Imagine that

- You can have whatever you want, whenever you want—no hassles, no obstructions, no barriers, no ifs or buts.
- Your access to everything you want is guaranteed and secure: you cannot lose the right to or the provision for everything you want, ever.
- No one can take away anything you want or need from you, ever.
- You don't gain anything by taking anything from anybody.

Will you struggle to be greater or better than someone else? Of course, No. If there is no insecurity, there cannot be a desire to be greater than others.

The need to be greater than others is very pronounced in competitive societies because the extent to which you are better or greater than others is the yardstick by which society measures your stature or place in it and what you can or cannot get. The greater than others you are, the more you can get from the society.

Since this dimension of insecurity inevitably results in selfish and aggressive behaviors (you must promote and protect your own interests, and find ways to bring others down so that you can elevate yourself), very competitive societies will always be infested with high levels of selfishness and aggression. You cannot do very well, financially for example, in such environments if you fail to "look out for number one" and ruthlessly protect your own interests. Aggressive, selfish persons do better in competitive environments than non-aggressive, selfless individuals.

Need to be Greater

The desire for equality and fairness is the opposite of the need to be greater than others and/or the need to be in control of others. The more secure a person feels, the less the need to be greater or in predatory control of others and the more the desire for the equality of all and fairness. This desire is highest at very high sphericities and decreases as the sphericity decreases (φ_p being equal).

It is necessary to note here that some people may desire equality for all not because of the operation of their high sphericity but out of a desire to rise and be on top themselves. Others may fake it because it sounds more civilized and like the right thing to do when their behavior in their interactions with others show otherwise. Who doesn't want to be counted as being committed to equality, justice and fairness? That is why it is very necessary to use all the traits discussed in this model in deciding the actual sphericity of individuals. As human beings we are very good at deceiving ourselves that we want one thing when we really want the opposite. A person who scores as low sphericity in other traits cannot score as high sphericity here. What is important in deciding sphericity is behavior, not self-report.

We shall discuss the need to be greater than others further by examining the following:
1. Aggression towards others
2. Need to bring others down in order to elevate oneself
3. Prejudice
4. Jealousy and Envy
5. Need to outsmart others
6. Holier-than-thou

The variation of the above characteristics with λ_p is shown in Figure 8.1.

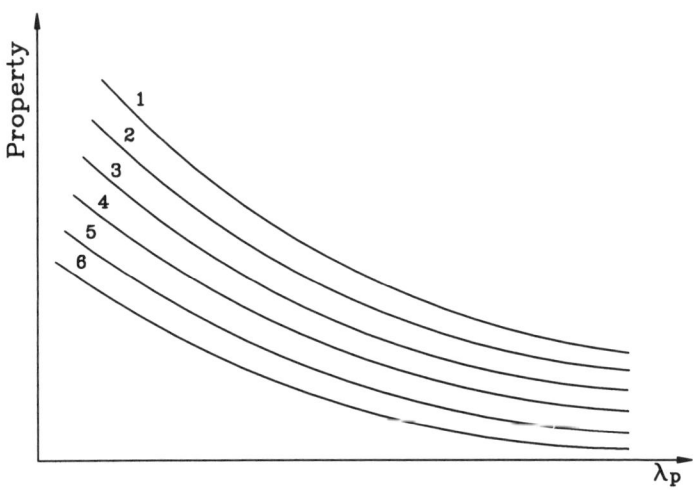

Figure 8.1. Variation of behavior with sphericity.

1. Aggression towards Others

Insecurity (frustration, pain, insults, uncomfortable temperatures, foul odors, etc. generate insecurity) creates anger which often provokes aggression. Most of our frustrations and pains come from other human beings, so we tend to take out our anger through aggressive behavior towards other people. Since we are all insecure in one degree or another, aggression is always a part of the human condition. Its occurrence and its intensity may vary from one social group to another depending on the values of the group, as we will see later, but it is always there (at least latently).

Lower sphericity individuals are more insecure than higher sphericity individuals and are therefore more aggressive. As suggested earlier, while biology (λ_p) disposes an individual to a degree of insecurity, the individual's environment (φ_p) also affects the feeling of insecurity and consequent aggression. The role of φ_p will be discussed more later.

A person may be very aggressive inwardly but may not show it if he lacks the strength to show it, so care must be taken in deciding whether a person is aggressive or not. Once he sees someone he thinks is weaker or lower than him, the aggressive side of his personality will explode like a volcanic eruption. Aggression may be verbal or physical—any form of wickedness against other people is aggression here.

The intensity of aggressive behavior is low in high sphericity individuals (because they feel more secure) and increases as the sphericity decreases. Low sphericity individuals can be rough, very rough, on their fellow human beings, higher sphericity individuals tend to be milder and softer—even when they have the power to show aggression.

2. Need to Bring Others Down in Order to Elevate Oneself

Insecurity leads one to feel very bad when he is dealt the low end, so he struggles to get the upper hand in every argument, in every encounter with his fellow man. Since the human mind has an irresistible urge to classify everything in greater/lower divisions, most competitive societies praise and reward those who are able to get the upper hand in human encounters—making aggressive behavior a part of everyday behavior.

Conquering the outer nature and making them serve us is not aggression in this definition but conquering other human beings is. Aggression is the desire to bring some human beings down so that one may be elevated, creating a dynamic that makes human life inescapably predatory and wicked.

If the desire to get an upper hand weren't that fierce and urgent, it would be easier to create conditions where everyone can find happiness. But our insecurities tell us that we cannot really be happy until others (whom we may refer to as competitors, opponents, colleagues, etc) are unhappy.

Insecurities lead to a philosophy of bankruptcy: We are not happy unless the next fellow is not. There isn't enough room for everyone to be happy and fulfilled, so I'd better pull the other person down so that I can set myself on high—and be "happy." In order for me to be happy (happiness is such a limited resource) I must make sure the other person is not.

A student is not happy with a 98% grade because everyone in the class scored more than 90%. He would be happier with 70% and every other person scoring less than 30%. Why? It gives him a feeling of superiority which calms the feelings (itching) of inadequacy that plague his fragile, insecure self. He is happy because he is "better" than the rest of the class (or because his classmates are unhappy). What a tragedy insecurity brings on human philosophy and psychology!

A professor presents his theory in such a complicated way that no one is sure he understands him. Why? He wants to show his audience that he is privy to some kind of secret, complex and advanced knowledge which they are ill-suited by their limited faculty to understand. The momentary feeling of superiority he derives from that alleviates (at least temporarily) the insecurity that hunts him day and night.

A psychotherapist is not happy that he is making over $400,000 a year until he learns that other professional psychologists are making $100,000 a year on the average. He is happy because he is "better" than the rest of his peers. And so on, and on, and on. How sweet it feels to our insecure selves to be on top and every one else below! Some would gladly kill just to experience that feeling.

This need to be greater, better, permeates every sphere of human activity, especially in competitive environments. It springs from our innate insecurity, our less-than-perfect sphericity. The higher the sphericity the lower the need to be greater than others (φ_p being equal).

It colors what we mean by achievement since societies measure success by this criterion. Achievement should mean mastery of circumstances and events to create something worthwhile for the entire race without tearing down any part of the society. Unfortunately, society defines success as anything that puts one on top of the pack. This philosophy is bound to ensure that aggression, crime, violence and wickedness will never be erased from human societies.

3. Prejudice

Groups behave like individuals. In every society, groups come up with a list of "traits" which make them superior to other groups. Every group does it. How could they be happy unless they can prove to themselves that there is something inherent in them that makes them superior to other groups? Philosophers, experts and other professionals quickly spring up to fill this enormous need. They show members of their group how they are better than others and why, and they quickly become famous and rich because the people have been yearning to hear just that (insecurity at work).

The result? Friction, misunderstanding, war, violence, etc. against the out-groups. After all what rights have those unfortunate souls to live side by side with superior people like us? Why can't they just accept the lot bestowed on them by "nature" and stop disturbing our peace?

Prejudice increases with a greater feeling of insecurity which increases as sphericity decreases (φ_p being equal). When a person is very insecure, he concentrates all his thoughts on his own survival. In other words, he becomes selfish, unable to consider the feelings of the other person. This is the root of prejudice and aggression towards people who are different from us. The intensity of prejudice is higher in lower sphericity individuals than in higher sphericity persons. Since competition makes life more insecure, the current of prejudice will be intense in competitive societies, especially among the more vulnerable lower classes.

4. Jealousy and Envy

Insecurity is the root of jealousy and envy. An envious person feels unhappy when his colleague, neighbor or peer seems to be progressing more than him. He may smile and congratulate him but inwardly he feels bad.

Jealousy is part of our need to be greater than others. We want to be greater than the next person so when he prospers more than us we become angry, jealous. It occurs in every human being because of our less-than-perfect sphericity but its intensity and frequency are higher in low sphericity individuals than in higher sphericity individuals.

5. Need to Outsmart Others

Our insecurities lead us to believe that every encounter with others is an opportunity to decide who is smarter, more intelligent, better than the other. Very insecure people (very low sphericity persons in this model) love to make fools of others, to deceive them and to show them that they are very smart, much smarter than them. More secure individuals, on the other hand, see little or no benefit in the dance of smartness.

6. Holier-than-thou

People do not seek more punishment for offenders (law breakers) because they think it is bad to commit offence (after all they all offend in one way or the other) but because it gives them a feeling that they are better than somebody; they may be bad, they will readily admit, but evidently not as bad as the real "bad" guys.

Lower λ_p persons (i.e. more insecure people) tend to seek more punishment for offenders than high λ_p individuals.

This holier-than-thou attitude (very pervasive in competitive societies) makes the politician who pledges to "fight" crime almost always more popular than one who promises to remove the causes of crime. People want all the "bad guys" to be put away. The trouble is, if we were actually able to put away all the bad guys, who would be left?

The more insecure a person feels the more he wants to know that he is holier than someone—that he is not all that bad despite all his crimes and wrong doings. As λ_p increases, this need decreases (φ_p being equal).

Summary

Low λ_p	High λ_p
1. Aggressive towards others	1. Mild and soft towards others
2. Need to bring others down in order to elevate oneself	2. Less need to bring others down
3. More susceptible to prejudice	3. Less susceptible to prejudice
4. Intensely jealous and envious of others' progress	4. Less jealous and envious of other people's progress
5. Love to outsmart and make fools of others	5. Little or no interest in outsmarting others
6. Wants to know he is "holier" than the next person	6. More likely to recognize the universality of evil

NOTE:

In a competitive society, if someone's φ_p is low and he doesn't have anyone to depend on (in other words, he is required to succeed but he is severely limited or handicapped by his φ_p), the resultant greater insecurity may make his need to be greater than someone run through the roof (more than his λ_p would naturally call for). When he meets someone who is weaker than him, the greatness of his need to trample on someone will be in full display. For this reason, violent aggression and heartless wickedness will be more common among lower class than among high class groups in a given competitive society.

As feminism erodes traditional male-female relationships (so that a woman does not have to depend on the man as before, for example), more and more women will become violently aggressive as they stand or fall on their own feet.

We suggest that to understand λ_p very well, φ_p should be considered.

Chapter Nine

Need for Emotional Expression

Life, especially other people, can be frustrating and annoying at times. Just when we think we have found a safe corner to rest our weary head, along come some disappointments and unnecessary provocations from the people we deal with.

These frustrations and disappointments aggravate our feelings of insecurity by increasing (or not decreasing) the difference between what we want and what we get. For those of us whose natural R is large (i.e. high sphericity individuals), this increase in potential difference does not often result in more current than our system can accomodate but for those of us with small R (i.e. low sphericity persons) such increases in potential difference overload our system and trip our fuse so that we lose control of our actions.

Our ability to control our response to our feelings and our actions during such trying circumstances is our measure of self-control or emotional expressiveness. Individuals with high self-control (high λ_p) can control their emotions or feelings better than emotionally expressive persons (low λ_p). Self-controlled people are ruled by their heads and react coolly, emotional expressive persons are ruled by their feelings and respond spontaneously to emotions or feelings. We shall examine the need for emotional expression under the following headings:

    1. Critical frustration level
    2. Emotional control
    3. Caution
    4. Self-assurance

The general variations of these with λ_p are shown in Figure 9.1.

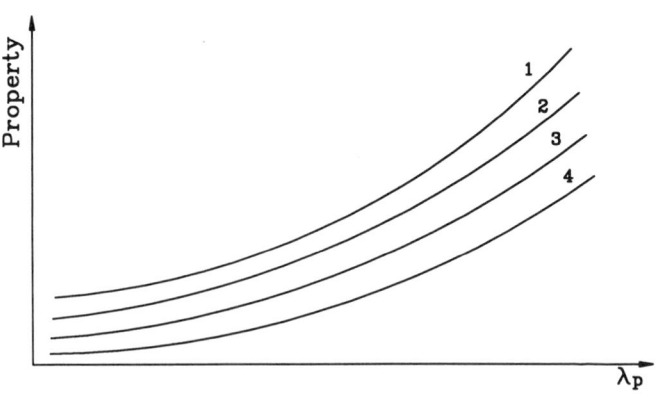

Figure 9.1. Variation of behavior with sphericity.

Need for Emotional Expression

1. Critical Frustration Level

Critical frustration level here means the amount of frustration any individual can take before losing his "cool." The greater the self-control a person has, the higher the critical frustration level. High sphericity individuals typically have higher critical frustration levels than lower sphericity persons. They can tolerate more flak or rude behavior from others. While we all boil over once in a while, the boiling points of these individuals are so high that it takes a lot of "heat" to bring them to a boil—even in cases where an angry outburst would not take away any privileges from them. The kind of annoying situations that would make a low sphericity person plot, do or say unthinkable things will hardly amount to any significance to a very high sphericity individual. They have higher frustration thresholds because they are less insecure—their R is so large that they can resist the generation of insecurity by potential differences better.

Being fiercely self-sufficient, as we saw, high λ_p persons find it hard to tolerate regulations they dislike. Their critical frustration level may be low here and high elsewhere.

2. Emotional Control

High sphericity individuals have higher emotional control than low sphericity individuals. It is difficult for the emotions of anger, sexual urge and appetite, for example, to overwhelm these souls. They are usually low, relatively speaking, in sexual interests and not very romantic. They are also almost always in control of their emotions due to their large R—making their lives very monotonous and dull.

Lower sphericity individuals, on the other hand, have a harder time (relatively speaking) controlling their emotions. Their emotional responses (anger, sexual urge, appetite, etc.)

are often intense and radioactive. In other words, they are emotionally expressive. They will go the distance to express how they feel or reserve the feelings for later expression. If thwarted or simply annoyed, for example, they may lash out harshly and sometimes violently against those causing them pain. They can fly into rage at the drop of a hat. Temper tantrums directed at their families and friends are therefore common. A high λ_p individual will find life with very emotionally expressive persons stormy, considering that their emotional reactions tend to come in the order of thunders and lightnings. Once relieved of their emotional build-up, however, they become nice and normal again.

Emotionally expressive individuals express their love like their anger: intensely. Because of their chronic feelings of emptiness or insecurity, due to their small R, they seem to live for love. Very romantic, seductive and sometimes flirtatious, they tend to be excellent lovers.

We all express our emotions at one time or another. High λ_p persons have more control on their emotions than low λ_p individuals because they are relatively more secure. Please note that very low λ_p persons, as we saw before, exercise caution in their lives as part of their self-defense strategy. If you are not careful you may be fooled into assigning high sphericity to them.

3. Caution

Self-controlled (high λ_p) people rule their lives with caution. Because they have access to a higher degree of self-mastery (due to their large R) than the rest of us, they are almost always able to weigh their plans and activities carefully. But sometimes they weigh too much and thus become indecisive. Always cautious to hang all the data together and avoid mistakes, they typically take longer to come to a definite decision—especially in narrow-view domain problems where they are not strongly gifted. For example, they may find it difficult to throw away items that have ceased to be useful, hoping that they may still find some use somewhere. Emotionally expressive persons (low λ_p) tend to be more decisive. The indecisiveness discussed above is different from another kind of indecisiveness usually seen in people with a high need to avoid reality (low λ_p). In the latter case, indecisiveness proceeds from a desire to avoid making a decision, to let someone else take the decision and be responsible for the consequences.

The cautionary tendencies of high λ_p persons make them pay too much attention to details. They check and recheck everything to make sure there are no flaws. Lower λ_p individuals are more realistic than idealistic. Note that persons with a high need for self-defense (very low λ_p individuals) also tend to pay attention to details but not for the same reasons as high λ_p persons.

4. Self-assurance

People who score high on the self-control trait (high sphericity individuals) have a degree of self-assurance that few of us know. They are so sure of themselves that they let their inner minds control their experiences of life. Exuberantly self-confident they are eternal optimists, believing that they can overcome their difficulties. When a difficult task, project or challenge shows up at their door, they almost always take a hopeful outlook—they have mastered themselves and they can master their tasks too. They may actually enjoy the difficulty of difficult challenges. Self-confident people tend to be good at many disciplines (with the possible exceptions of sociability and group games). We all have a measure of self-confidence but some of us have more than others. Please note that self-confidence is not the same thing as self-esteem.

Summary

Low λ_p	High λ_p
1. Low critical frustration level	1. High critical frustration level
2. Ruled by feelings, respond spontaneously to emotions	2. Ruled by reason, respond coolly to emotions
3. Low emotional control	3. High emotional control
4. Temper tantrums and angry outbursts	4. Little or no angry outbursts
5. Expressive lovers	5. Cold, unexpressive lovers
6. More decisive	6. Less decisive
7. Realistic and pragmatic	7. Idealistic and perfectionistic

NOTE:

As we will see in later chapters, low φ_p adds so much more frustrations and disappointments to a person's life that he will more likely be more emotionally expressive (especially the emotion of anger) than someone with a similar λ_p but higher φ_p. That is why we emphasize in this book that to obtain a good portrait of λ_p, φ_p should be accounted for.

Chapter Ten

Speed of Response to Motivation

We are discussing human psychological realities here by comparing them to insights obtained from the physical world of particles. Particles respond at varying "speeds" to force or flow. We expect human beings also to respond to motivation at varying speeds if our analogy is any good. There is evidence that this is so. We shall examine this further by examining the following:
    1. Ease and intensity of dynamic arousal
    2. Ease of initiative display
    3. Speed of thinking and acting
    4. Singleness of purpose

94 Portraits of Excellence

5. Persistent devotion to work
6. Ability to follow twists and turns

The general variations of these characteristics with λ_p are shown in Figure 10.1.

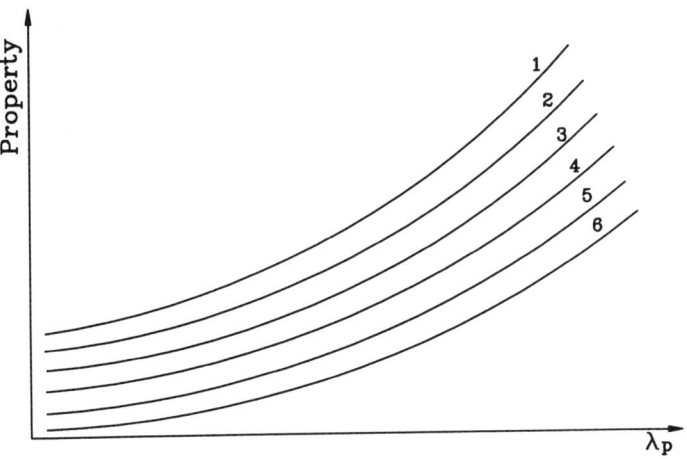

Figure 10.1. Variation of behavior with sphericity.

1. Ease and Intensity of Dynamic Arousal

The more spherical a particle is, the faster or easier it moves in response to a force or flow. Imagine two particles, one spherical and the other of irregular shape. When you try to move both particles with a stream of air, you will find that the spherical particle starts moving with a lower air velocity than the irregularly shaped (less spherical) particle. At equal air velocities you will find that the spherical particle moves more "intensely" than the irregularly shaped particle.

Higher sphericity makes a particle more susceptible to changes in its flow or force environment. Less spherical particles are less responsive and therefore less movable.

The same sort of thing occurs in human behavior. High sphericity individuals are more easily and intensely aroused by flow (desire, idea) than low sphericity individuals. Once an idea or desire catches their fancy they tend to go with it almost spontaneously, unreservedly. They quickly pour their energy and zeal into the idea or desire with such intensity that we would be hard put to express in words. In other words, they are dynamically impulsive but not emotionally impulsive. They can usually control their bodily emotions (anger, sex, etc.) but once an idea has taken hold of them, they let it drive them, just like physical particles.

We are all driven at one time or another but the level of individual dynamic impulsiveness varies—from high in high sphericity individuals to low in low sphericity individuals. Dynamic impulsiveness results in a number of problems in people who score high on this dimension:

      (i) Dynamic impulsiveness sometimes leads to serious errors in judgment.

      (ii) It may lead to a loss of face, when the end result shows that the person has acted too quickly.

      (iii) It may lead to too much variations in a person's way of expending limited energy and resources.

For example, a dynamically impulsive individual may start on a project when he does not have the necessary experience and resources to bring it to a fruitful end. Just as he is realizing his error, another idea presents itself, he jumps into it, discovers later he was unwise again, jumps into another, etc., etc. In other words, it could make a person appear foolish, inconsistent, drifting and uncalculating.

But this kind of flexibility enables him to keep coming at a problem from a variety of angles using a variety of techniques and hence arrive at breakthrough solutions faster than the rest of us. It also makes his mind ever receptive and plastic. When his sense of what is going on with his idea or around him bids him give up the immediate battle and start afresh on some new line, he makes the switch quite fast.

The great advantage of dynamic impulsiveness, however, is that it could land a person in places where no human being has ever been before. Because of the ease and intensity with which the individual is aroused, he can take on "impossible" projects without knowing that they are impossible. Sometimes he wins and his victory becomes an advance for mankind. For this reason and others, most great discoveries and achievements will be made by people who score high on dynamic impulsiveness. They are the natural (mostly non-political) leaders of the human race, even though they don't appear to be very wise, in this author's opinion.

It makes sense that high λ_p individuals are dynamically impulsive. Since they feel less insecure than the rest of us, they can give themselves completely to their flow more readily than low λ_p persons. Low λ_p individuals are too insecure to attempt that. They will need assurance that the way is clear before they can comfortably set sail. Even when they are on their way their insecurities wisely advise them to leave one hand in their pockets in case something happens. High λ_p persons do not have that much insecurity to instruct them, so they plunge ahead, not knowing what lies ahead except that their high self-confidence assures them that they will come out alright. Sometimes they do, sometimes they don't.

2. Ease of Initiative Display

Another characteristic that accompanies being easily and intensely aroused, is a high degree of initiative display. People who score high on dynamic impulsiveness are easily moved to take action in the direction of their desires. They get up and start doing something almost as soon as they are overtaken by an idea or desire. Some of us give it sometime before committing an initiative to it, others try to avoid doing anything. The higher the sphericity the higher the degree of initiative display.

3. Speed of Thinking and Acting

As we have seen, a relatively low level of velocity is enough to send a spherical particle zooming into places it has never been before. Dynamically impulsive individuals are so intensely aroused by their ideas or desires, that they think and act at great speed.

Depending on our skills and experience on certain subjects we all tend to think and act at great speed but high sphericity individuals are characteristically different. If you are around them, you can feel the intensity of the desires that is being displayed in the speed of their thoughts and actions.

4. Singleness of Purpose

The more perfectly shaped (spherical, in our case), the more uniform and unidirectional the flow lines around the particle, everything being equal (see Figure 10.2). With lower sphericity there are more diversions and crookedness in the flow lines.

A similar thing occurs among the human population. We have already seen that high sphericity individuals have strong,

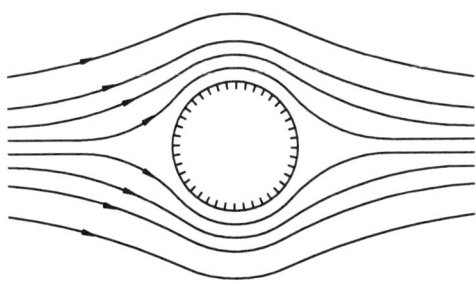

Figure 10.2. Flow lines around a particle.

intense arousals just like high sphericity particles in physical flow. Their flow lines are also more unidirectional than others, just like physical particles. This expresses itself in singleness of purpose in the individual. High sphericity individuals are typically devoted entirely to one cause to the exclusion of almost every other concern. They are owned and driven by their causes or projects, instead of the other way round. Once they step into flow in a particular direction, they become fanatically devoted to it and other aspects of their lives—their social lives, relationships, etc., start to suffer. They are not very good at taking it easy—everything is done intensely, with excessive zeal, concentration and devotion. Lower λ_p persons are better at taking it easy at work and exploring other areas of their lives while doing their work. They are less single-eyed.

5. Persistent Devotion to Work

Strong, intense arousals and singleness of purpose point to one thing: persistent devotion to work. Spherical particles are more in tune with "their" flow. They are totally devoted to the cause of their flow; nothing is important as their work, project or idea. They are willing to expend every fiber of their being to turn in a clean, thorough and complete job. Every discussion, every activity is carried on and its value determined by their relevance to their work. Work becomes the central domain, the control center, of every experience and activity. Such devotion to duty will make most of us despair of life but to very high sphericity individuals it is the stuff that happiness is made of. They enjoy work, finding it liberating, exhilarating and immensely satisfying or fulfilling. Don't tell them that there is more to life than work because they won't be able to comprehend you, let alone value your helping spirit. Lower λ_p persons tend to know how to balance life and work.

6. Ability to Follow the Twists and Turns

As can be seen in physical flow systems, spherical particles follow the twists and turns in their flow path better than irregularly shaped particles, everything being equal. High sphericity individuals are similarly better than low sphericity people in following the twists and turns of fortune. They tend to have more psychological resources and equipment for surviving failures and hostile circumstances than less dynamically impulsive people (φ_p being equal). Criticisms, obstacles, hurdles are rarely able to stop these ever-rolling stones (unless in cases where their φ_p is terribly low).

Summary

Low λ_p	High λ_p
1. Dynamically less impulsive	1. Dynamically more impulsive
2. Less likely to have an initiative	2. More likely to have an initiative
3. Less likely to think and act at great speed	3. More likely to think and act at great speed
4. Less single-eyed	4. More single-eyed
5. Less persistent devotion to work	5. More persistent devotion to work
6. Less likely to follow twists and turns of fortune well	6. More likely to follow twists and turns of fortune well

NOTE:

Low φ_p does not leave enough margins for a person to take risks or to survive or persevere through harsh situations like someone with equal λ_p but higher φ_p. In other words, low φ_p lowers dynamic impulsiveness and perseverance. Therefore, for us to understand λ_p in relation to response to motivation, we need to account for φ_p. φ_p is discussed further later.

Chapter Eleven

Classification of Individuals On The λ_p Scale

The seven factors discussed above: need for self-defense, breadth of view, need to avoid reality, need for others, need to be greater than others, need for emotional expression, and speed of response to motivation represent bundles of some of the psychological behavior of human beings. These "traits" can be plotted on the sphericity of particles as continuous functions. Other factors can easily be plotted on the sphericity frame also, because human behavior relates to human sphericity, their inadequacies or insecurities (remember this was our central principle in the beginning). Instead of traits dangling in free air, they are tied down to a reliable frame of reference in the physical domain, making their determination and study more objective and concrete.

Once the traits are plotted on the sphericity frame, the personalities of individuals can be fixed on the graph. Personalities can be classified into a thousand or a million categories or to one, two or ten, etc—any number that the researcher or scientist wants.

To demonstrate our theory, in this chapter we shall divide the human population into eight personalities and see how our traits describe them. Why eight? No special reason.

All we want to do here is to show that the better portrait obtained using our looking-glass theory can be used in the classification of individual behavior if such a classification is needed.

Please note that the personalities presented in this chapter are theoretically determined. Until specific experiments are done to confirm or verify them, they are only useful as theories. Secondly, φ_p is not yet discussed, so keep an opening for environmental or social influences as you evaluate these theories.

The eight groups are shown below and in Figure 11.1 on the λ_p frame of reference.

Group	Broad category	Dominant trait(s)
1. Vigilant, Smart	Extraverted	η_{sd}
2. Suspicious, Easy-going	Extraverted	η_{sd}/η_{ar}
3. Adventurous, Bold	Extraverted	η_{ar}/η_{fo}

Classification on λ_p Scale

4. Party, Center stage — Extraverted — η_{fo}/η_{ar}
5. People, Caring — Extraverted — η_{fo}
6. Prestige, Power — Extraverted — η_{go}
7. Caution, Work — Introverted — η_{ee}
8. Impulsive, Visionary — Introverted — η_{sr}

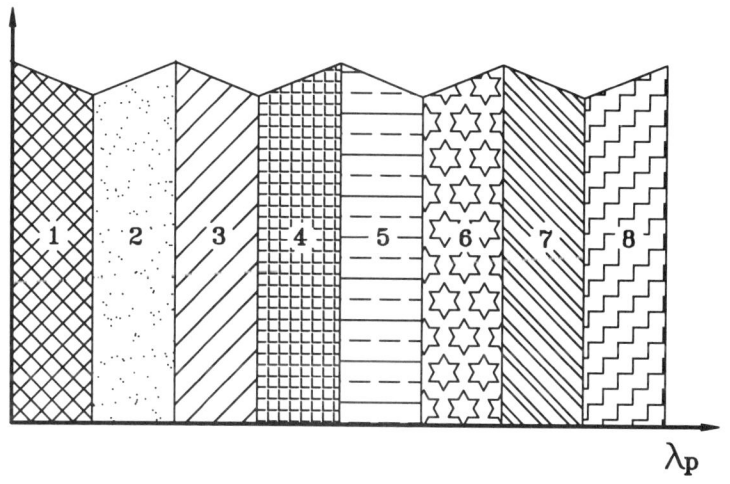

Figure 11.1. Personality groups in relation to sphericity.

Since we have discussed the traits before we shall describe the groups just briefly. With knowledge of the traits and the sphericity scale we are using, it is easy to place the groups once the facts are known.

Group 1. Vigilant, Smart

As you can see from Figure 11.1, Group 1 individuals are very high on the need for self-defense. They are the most insecure of the human population and the smartest. They are naturals in "looking out for number one" and are therefore bound to be successful in competitive environments, if their φ_p is not limiting.

They are also high in the need of others, in the desire to escape reality, the need to pull others down, but the dominant trait here is the need for self-defense. Their most salient characteristics have already been discussed.

Group 1 individuals have relatively extraordinary desires to protect themselves from the "hostile, evil" world around them. Consumed with mistrust, they believe that other people mean them harm. Owing to this, they are usually exceptionally aware of their environment. Smart, vigilant people tend to be very secretive, subtle, tactful and self-orientedly diplomatic in their dealings with others. They are almost always hiding one aspect or the other of their lives from others as part of their general self-defense duties. They are very good at perceiving mixed messages, hidden motivations, subtle dishonesties, evasions, etc.

In defense of their very fragile egos (high levels of insecurity), they don't like their errors to be pointed out, ever. They are extremely touchy about criticism and it is almost impossible for them to accept blame. It is always someone else who should be blamed for their apparent misdeeds, not them. They are simply never "wrong." Group 1 individuals are usually very prone to jealousy, envy, prejudice and hate. They hate to see others progress more than themselves or even do well at all. Smart, vigilant managers, you will find, hate to see their subordinates move up in the organization, for

Classification on λ_p Scale

no rational reason. They can also be very vindictive, unforgiving and hypersensitive to the tiniest insults.

Smart, vigilant people are extraordinarily good at arguments. They have a special knack for noticing weak points in their opponent's line of argument—a testament to their ever watchful style of life. While they are not good at broadview, abstract-level arguments, they are unbeatable in the small stuff of day-to-day living—and most of our everyday life activities revolve on small stuff! Their guarded or watchful style of life makes them appear introverted (as defined in this model) but they are not. They keep away from others not because they don't really need them (like real introverts) but because they fear that others are out to get them—to avoid giving somebody an opportunity to take advantage of them. They appear very confident, independent, tough, and assertive.

Group 2. Suspicious, Easy-going

Group Two individuals are also high on mistrust and suspicion but not as high as Group One. They are usually easy-going individuals who don't especially like work but will do what they have to do to earn their living. If their job is typing a document, they will do just that. Don't expect them to "clean up" your files for you; that is not their job.

They love pleasure, pampering and loving attention. How great they would feel if someone else undertook to take care of their needs while they sit around and watch soap-operas with a favorite bag of chips at their reach. Being very self-oriented, smart, and tactful they would not put the needs of others, their relationships and their work before their personal pleasure.

They don't want to be driven by the clock (time). They want to take it easy and enjoy their lives without being enslaved by time or work. Because of their focus on enjoying life, they will not drive hard to achieve success or fame. They are happy with their piece of the action. They will work to get money to meet their needs, for pension, etc. but they won't "kill themselves" to achieve what the capitalistic society calls success. They love to avoid obligations or responsibilities if they can. They will procrastinate until the last minute—but they seem to pull through fine.

The need for others is very high in Group 2 individuals; it is not buried by suspicion as in Group One individuals. They tend to enter relationships easily but they will never sacrifice their personal pleasure. They will not run with the clock even if that is what the person in their lives appreciate. Their high self-orientedness makes them very skilled at saying no to demands they think are unreasonable or above and beyond the call of duty. Usually cooperative, good workers, they don't take work home. There is a time and place for everything. Work when you have to, treat yourself to some pleasure at other times. Like Group One individuals, they are prone to jealousy, envy, prejudice and hate, but less intense than Group One. They are also vindictive and find it very hard to accept blame.

Group 3. Adventurous, Bold

Adventurous individuals have a healthy disrespect for reality. They would venture where most mortals fear to tread and try to ignore reality whenever they can. The dominant trait of this group is found in the need to avoid or ignore reality. They do this through thrill and sensation seeking and by being reckless with drugs, alcohol, gambling, money, sex, and the law. Always hungry for peak experiences and excitement, Group 3 individuals tend to be mischief makers with little or no remorse for their deeds, especially when their φ_p is low.

Very self-oriented, smart and bold, they use their natural smartness and persuasiveness to win friends or to con people. They are also emotionally expressive. If annoyed they often react harshly or violently against people causing them pain. Being low in emotional control, they are easily ruled by drugs, alcohol, or sex (they love varieties of sexual experience). But for their emotional instability and planlessness, they tend to be excellent salespeople, actors, politicians and writers.

Group 4. Party, Center Stage

Group Four individuals are also sensation lovers who need lots of praise and attention from others to assure them that all is well with them. They love parties, high degrees of excitement, and meeting new friends. They pay lots of attention to their grooming and clothes—they love it when all eyes on them. Naturally good at reading people and body language like Groups One, Two and Three, they are great at charming people, selling, promoting, wheeling and dealing, and of course, acting. Group Four individuals like those of Group 3 are not high on emotional or self-control; they tend to be weak when it comes to controlling their appetites, sexual urges, hot tempers, keeping secrets, etc. They make great actors, excellent salespeople, corporate executives and charismatic leaders.

Group 5. People, Caring

Group 5 individuals are people who need attention, love, and approval from people but not to the extent of Group 4 individuals. They are more interested in approval from familiar sources—family and friends. They need less excitement than Group 4 individuals and love it when things are settled into routine, with everyone knowing what is expected from him or her. They care deeply about what other people (a small territory consisting of their friends and acquaintances) think about them, so they work very hard to win their approval and avoid criticism. They tend to be loyal to their family and friends. Politely reserved but nonetheless extraverted (as defined in this model), they move into new situations with caution and emotional reserve. They find new situations stressful until they are familiar with them. They do well in jobs requiring repetition, habit and routine.

Group 6. Prestige, Power

Group 6 individuals are people whose greatest need is to be greater than everyone else, to dominate and rule others, to get an edge over others, etc. The need to be greater than others is also great (even greater, potentially) in Groups 1 to 5 individuals but other needs like security, excitement and approval from others tend to mask it. In Group 6, the need to defend the self, for sensation and for love from others are not as high, so the need to rule becomes dominant. These status, prestige and power seekers are naturals at understanding the power structures in their organization. They know which route leads to what and they work hard to unseat those above them and cut off those who may be interested in the office they seek. With more self-control and endurance than Groups 1 to 5, they are goal-oriented and very disciplined in their lives, milking people and events for all they are worth. Shrewd, extraverted and competitive, they make good politicians and corporate executives.

Group 7. Caution, Work

Group 7 individuals are introverted, us-oriented individuals of very high moral principles. Being low on self-oriented interests, they find fulfillment at work—solving

Classification on λ_p Scale

problems that need to be solved at work and in the community. They work very hard, not to obtain the praise of others (although that wouldn't hurt) but for pleasure—they derive tremendous pleasure and release from work. The problem at work or in the community gives them a need towards which they can release their humanity since they don't seem to have gnawing needs of their own like the rest of us. Hard work becomes the hallmark of their personality. Emotionally controlled, hungers (appetite), sexual urges and hot tempers do not often get the best of them. They tend to overdose on details—their standards tend to be too high, in this author's opinion. As you would expect, they are not very romantic and their love life is treated much like work: in a cold, calculated, reason-controlled, boring manner (someone should tell them that love and reason do not go together—love is a feeling, not an exercise in reasoning). But if you can endure a monotonous, less romantic love life, these are the most loyal, dedicated lovers you can find. They will hang in with you through thick and thin, and take care of you as no one else can.

Group 8. Impulsive, Visionary

Group 8 individuals are very much like people in Group 7, differing only in degrees. They are practically very low on the passionate need for others and do very well (and prefer to be) alone or with very few close relationships. They have very few needs that are self-oriented and their primary goal in life is to be helpful to others—to work for the greater good of all. Out of deference to and respect for others, they will seek to achieve their goals without harming or destroying another person. Always considerate of others and ready to excuse their weaknesses and foibles, Group 8 individuals are as kind, forgiving, honest and trustworthy as these can get. Consequently they tend to be naive and unprepared for the real world where underhandedness and trickery are part of the game. As can be seen from their location on our graph, these individuals are dynamically impulsive (not emotionally impulsive, ever), driven by a single purpose at a time, visionary (broadviewed) and will tend to be trail blazers for mankind in philosophical reasoning and intellectual creativity. But this author thinks that most people with this style of personality will find life very frustrating unless they learn to be selfish as much as they can. It is good to seek the greater good but a good sprinkling of selfishness and wickedness will not hurt.

Chapter Twelve

Environmental Empowerment Factor

The other important factor that affects the movement of the particle is the environmental empowerment factor φ_p. In the physical domain it represents the momentum imparted to the particle causing it to move in a certain direction.

The psychology of human beings, we have seen, is manifested only during those times that the human particle is living, moving and interacting with the people and the world around him. We have also seen how the physical characteristics of the particle that affect its motion is analogous to the biological foundations of human psychology. In this section, we will examine how another factor that influences particle motion, φ_p, relates to human psychological behavior.

Particle momentum, φ_p

Imagine that there is a particle in front of an opening to a large tank of particles as sketched in Figure 12.1. A force F is acting on the particle and moving it through the opening into the large tank. You don't need to be a physicist to know that the velocity with which the particle enters and travels in the tank as well as how far it penetrates into the established pack of particles depend on the force F. If F is very large, the particle will smash its way through the pack. If F is small or weak, the particle will have to content itself with a position in the sidelines in the tank.

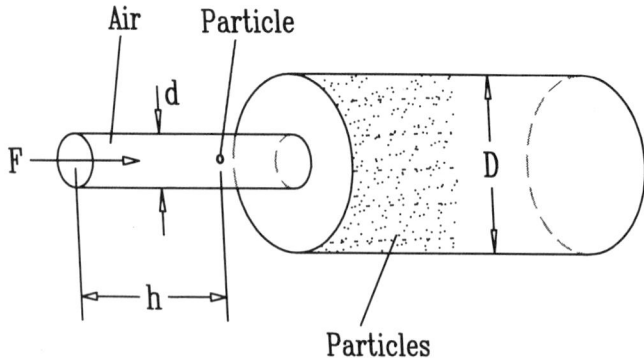

Figure 12.1. Particle movement in relation to group.

Environmental Empowerment 113

Before we continue, let's make it clear that Figure 12.1 is analogous to the human condition. The particle is the individual wanting to get into the world of people (this is essentially how each individual sees himself in relation to the world—outside).

Now let's get back to the particle and Figure 12.1. We will attempt to refresh our memory that force is the rate of change of momentum, so that we can see clearly where our φ_p comes from. From elementary science we know that force is mass multiplied by acceleration:

$$F = ma \qquad (12.1)$$

where:
    F is the force
    m is the mass
    a is the acceleration

Acceleration is the rate of change of velocity (i.e. the difference between the final velocity and the initial velocity divided by the time elapsed between them).

$$a = (V - U)/t \qquad (12.2)$$

where:
    V is the final velocity
    U is the initial velocity
    t is the time

If we put the value of a (the acceleration) in equation 12.2 in equation 12.1 we'll get

$$F = m(V-U)/t \qquad (12.3)$$

If the initial velocity U = 0 (i.e. the particle is at rest until F came along)

$$F = m(V/t) \qquad (12.4)$$

or

$$F = mV/t \qquad (12.5)$$

If we hold the time t constant in each case, F becomes the momentum transferred to the particle, allowing it to move. This momentum will occupy the bulk of our attention here. We shall designate the momentum as φ_p

$$\varphi_p = mV \qquad (12.6)$$

Notice that φ_p is a vector since V is a vector. For its specification we have to state both its magnitude (how much it is) and its direction (where it is headed).

In Figure 12.1 it is shown that the force F acting on the particle is exerted by the air in the conduit containing the particle. So the φ_p of the particle is the momentum imparted to it by the air

$$\varphi_p = \text{mass of air x velocity of air} \qquad (12.7)$$

Remember that the density (and mass) of the particles we are considering are not important (we assumed them to be irrelevant to our study in the beginning).

Relating this to the human particle, the air in Figure 12.1 represents the intangible influences in the individual's

empowering unit, represented by the conduit containing the particle.
The mass of air in the conduit is

$$\text{mass} = \text{density} \times \text{volume} \qquad (12.8)$$

Assume the density of air to be about unity and the volume of a cylinder is

$$\text{volume} = \pi\, d^2/4 \times h \qquad (12.9)$$

so

$$\text{mass} = \pi\, d^2/4 \times h \qquad (12.10)$$

Assume that h is same for everyone i.e. everyone starts out at the same point. Every human being starts experiencing the world around him at birth; what vary are the circumstances into which one is born and the nature of each individual.
Therefore

$$\varphi_p = \pi\, d^2/4\; V \qquad (12.11)$$

Since we are not interested in absolute values but in comparing cases to one another, we will simply say that

$$\varphi_p = d^2\, V \qquad (12.12)$$

To avoid dealing with units (like m, m/s, etc), let's make d dimensionless by referring it to D in Figure 12.1 and V to V_t

$$\varphi_p = d^2/D^2 \ V/V_t \qquad (12.13)$$

where:
 d is the size of the individual's empowering unit
 D is the size of the relevant society
 V is the motivation vector
 V_t is the terminal velocity of the particle being moved

Nothing has changed. φ_p is still a function of the product of d^2 and V but they are now expressed dimensionlessly.

In the physical system, once we know the values of d, D, V and V_t we can calculate or estimate φ_p. The same procedure applies to our human particle. Let's start by defining what we mean by d, D, V and V_t with respect to the individual.

d is the size of the individual's private empowering unit. It represents all the intangible and sometimes tangible things that combine to empower or disempower the individual. We will come back to it later.

D is the size of the society or group in which the individual wishes to move, interact and fulfil his purposes. For each case where φ_p is needed in this model, D will be same for all individuals, unless otherwise stated.

V is the motivation vector. It represents the intensity (magnitude) and direction of the motivating force the individual is exposed to.

V_t is the terminal velocity of the individual. It stands for the minimum velocity required for the particle to be air-borne (pneumatically transported by the motivating force). It depends on the shape of the particle in this model (every other characteristic is held constant, you remember). Spherical particles have lower terminal velocities than irregularly shaped particles. This means that high sphericity individuals have lower terminal velocities than low sphericity individuals. High sphericity individuals are therefore more readily carried away (air-borne) by their motivating force than low sphericity individuals. The same motivating force that could send high sphericity individuals flying may not even be felt by low sphericity individuals.

The use of V_t here is an assumption that nature and nurture come together in the empowerment factor. In other words, the empowerment a particle can receive from its environment depends on the kind of environment and the nature of the particle. Different particles respond differently to the same environment.

To make equation 12.13 easier to write and remember, let's replace d^2/D^2 with d_e and V/V_t with V_m. Therefore

$$\varphi_p = d_e\, V_m \quad\quad\quad (12.14)$$

Now, we'll look at d_e and V_m, one after the other.

Size Of The Empowering Unit, d_e

$$d_e = d^2/D^2 \quad\quad\quad (12.15)$$

As equation 12.15 shows, the size of the empowering unit, d_e, is the size of the intangible as well as tangible factors in the individual's world that combine to empower or disempower him with respect to the relevant society or group.

What makes up the empowering unit will differ from case to case since different situations require different sets of resources for proper handling. In general, we would suggest, there are about eight factors that are prominent in most cases: Attitude, Skills, Knowledge, Money, Equipment, Time, People, and Social fund.

$$d_e = f(ASK\ MET\ PF) \quad (12.16)$$

where:
- A stands for Attitude
- S stands for Skills
- K stands for Knowledge
- M stands for Money
- E stands for Equipment
- T stands for Time
- P stands for People (connections)
- F stands for Social fund
- f stands for "function of"

Motivation Vector, V_m

$$V_m = V/V_t \quad (12.17)$$

The motivation vector, V_m, is the intensity of the motivation driving the individual in the direction of the force. It is a ratio of the motivation velocity the individual is exposed to, V, to his or her responsiveness, V_t.

High sphericity individuals respond more to the same V than low sphericity individuals because their V_t is lower (V must be in the same direction of interest to all the particles being compared). Take two particles as examples:

Particle (a) $V = 15$ m/s
$V_t = 5$ m/s
$V_m = 15/5 = 3$

Particle (b) $V = 15$ m/s
$V_t = 10$ m/s
$V_m = 15/10 = 1.5$

So for the same V, particle (a) is twice as motivated as particle (b). Human biological nature play a big role in the individual's motivational characteristics.

Chapter Thirteen

The Empowering Unit

In the last chapter we saw that the size of the empowering unit, de, is the size of the intangible as well as tangible factors in the individual's world that combine to empower or disempower him or her with respect to the relevant society or group.

We also saw that about eight factors are prominent in the make-up of the empowering unit:
    1. Attitude (Self-esteem),
    2. Skills,
    3. Knowledge,
    4. Money,

5. Equipment,
6. Time,
7. People, and
8. Social fund.

In this chapter we shall look at each of these factors separately.

1. Attitude (Self-esteem)

Imagine that the components of an individual's environment can be represented as three concentric pipes as shown in Figure 13.1.

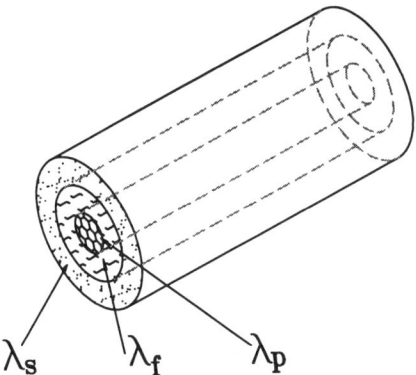

Figure 13.1. The individual in relation to society.

λ_p represents the individual, λ_f represents his family and λ_s represents the society. To bring out the role of each of these components clearly, let's take 'a traveller to a strange land' analogy. In this analogy, λ_s is the strange land with established language, values, routes and sites unknown to the traveller. λ_f is the guide and interpreter. λ_p is the traveller himself.

As we saw when we discussed the starting point of the individual in society, we all come into the world as strangers. The world was already here before we arrived. Society had already decided what is important and what is not; what is good and what is bad. We come in completely unprepared for this experience except for some genetic codes imprinted in us by our biology. We are expected to live and work in this strange land for some years and then vanish.

First, we need to understand the language of this strange people we'll be living with. Then we need to form our own opinion (an expression of our master survival plan) of what this strange land is and how we should proceed to make our temporary stay enjoyable and memorable. This opinion will form our general attitude to life in the strange land.

Three things go into the formation of this opinion or attitude:

1. Our own nature—what we like and what we dislike. In other words, our λ_p. If we like the values of the people of the strange land, our attitude to life will be different than if we find many of their values less than desirable or downright disgusting. Our own experiences in the strange land will affect our attitude.

2. The nature and "opinion" of our guide and interpreter, λ_f. If our guide told us that the strange land is a wonderful land of opportunity where we can make it big, chances are that our opinion of the land would be different than if he told us that it is a land of poisonous snakes and that we'll have to concentrate our energies on avoiding these venomous beasts.

We would also watch, take clues from and try to model our guide and interpreter—after all he's been here much longer and understands the culture and the landscape of the strange land very well. The survival skills we develop and the direction we take will be greatly influenced by our guide.

3. The nature of the strange land, λ_s. If it is a land of peace and safety, our opinion would be different than if it is a land seeded with explosive mines and warring factions.

The society sets the general tone for everyone living in it, whether the individual likes it or not. Plato said that what is honored in a society will be grown there.

As Kluckhohn (1949) wrote: "Culture regulates our lives at every turn. From the moment we are born until we die there is, whether we are conscious of it or not, constant pressure upon us to follow certain types of behavior that other men have created for us" (p.327).

Society determines the status of individuals, the roles each individual performs, the duties they are bounded by, the privileges they enjoy, how they perceive themselves and others, and how they earn and spend money.

A society that makes us aware of how we differ from others and heightens our sense of individuality would affect our attitude differently than an environment that places a strong emphasis on conformity. An urbanized, capitalistic society would present a different picture of life to us than a socialist, humane society.

As we touched upon earlier, the society also presents to each individual a picture of how he should view himself: race, sex, status, and what to expect as a consequence of belonging to any of these socially derived categories. Rosenberg (1979) wrote, "The broader society responds to people not so much in terms of what they are as in terms of [certain] categories. People may look with respect on a professor (though he be a dunce), show disdain toward a black (though he be a genius), express fear and distrust of an ex-convict (though he be scrupulously honest), feel uneasiness toward a released mental patient; and so on" (p.12).

As the guide and interpreter, the family prepares the individual for λ_s by providing him with an operational base, values and models for understanding and surviving in the society. It provides the traveller with love, approval, attention, survival equipment and training, feedback and a cushion against harsh realities of social life which the individual has not experienced before.

The family may affect the individual's attitude to life by stimulating the individual's interests in certain matters, transmitting societal values and knowledge, and providing access to the necessary materials for exercising skills valuable in the society. As Faris (1969) wrote, "We may also look within family processes to find how it comes about that some children gain a self-concept of a person who expects to be able to do whatever he decides to undertake" (p.25).

A person can still make it without a family but the odds will be piled against him. Life on earth is hard. To confront it head on without the cushionary and interpretative intervention of a family is to be at a real disadvantage, to say the least. It is not a recommended route.

The social identity elements, the general nature of the society, the nature of his family experiences, and his biological nature combine to determine a person's self-esteem—what he believes is his role in life and whether he views himself as being able to successfully master certain challenges or not.

A person's attitude and self-esteem determine which skills and knowledge he draws into himself and how efficiently he utilizes his money (inherited or earned), the equipment or tools at his disposal, his time, the people around him, and his social fund to make his trip to the land of the living a good one for himself and for his fellow travellers.

2. Skills

Many years ago, Aristotle wrote that "the things we have to learn before we can do them, we learn by doing them." Skills are those things we learn by doing them. The "doing" aspect is what differentiates skills from knowledge. For example, a person may know computer programming but until he starts to write and run his own programmes he does not develop computer programming skills. Skills fall into about three major categories:
        (i) Life Skills
        (ii) Social Skills
        (iii) Specialized Skills

(i) Life Skills

Life skills are those skills that help us to manage ourselves in relation to the reality of our existence. Some of these are:

- **Approach to life**

No one comes equipped and prepared to handle the issues of life. A good approach to life has to be learned and actively applied until it becomes second nature. Those fortunate to be born to strong, stable families may gain this skill from their parents; others would have to develop an approach to life on their own or learn from others.

A good approach to life, as you might imagine, matters a great deal. Some think that a parent, a teacher, a friend, a boss, a spouse, the company they work for, or some governmental program should shoulder their burdens and turn their lives into what they want them to be but life simply doesn't work like that. Our contract with life demands that we live our lives ourselves, taking advantage of whatever help we can get but never fully depending on those advantages. Others think that they can just drift into great personal success but again life says no, that's not the way it works. As Hesiod (c. 700 B.C.) wrote: "In front of excellence the immortal gods have put sweat, and long and steep is the way to it."

There are several other ways that people misunderstand life and suffer for their ignorance which we don't have the time and the space to mention here. The important point we want to make is that life is a solo flight and everyone should develop his or her own approach to life—by logical reasoning, by trial and error, or by learning from others.

• Discipline

The most prominent or well-known life skill is discipline. Discipline refers to the management of our insecurity and natural inclinations which run counter to our goals. A disciplined life is a life that is governed by the individual living it. In order to succeed in our pursuit of happiness in this our brief stay on the conscious side of existence, we've got to struggle to be in control of our game, that's discipline. We must discipline ourselves to get up when we have to, work hard and achieve our dreams. No one else will do this for us. Discipline also means that we must push ourselves to do those things which we know are good for us but we hate to do. For example, if you are a salesman, you must go out everyday and sell whether you feel like it or not. You will be rejected many times and it will hurt you every time but you must keep pushing. That's the little price we pay for this wonderful experience of life.

- **Time Management Skills**

    Time is our most important resource and the asset we most often abuse. Like an ever-rolling stream, time is constantly driving us to the end of our trip to consciousness but we often don't know it. It appears to be an inexhaustible resource but it's not. Once passed it cannot be recalled. Our ability to manage the time we have on our hands will ultimately decide whether our quest for happiness and fulfillment is successful or not. How often we wonder where all the time we had had gone?

- **Talent Management Skills**

    No one is without a talent. As Lord Beaverbrook wrote, "Every man [and every woman, of course] can find a niche in the social order which he can successfully occupy." The trick is to find that niche early enough to do you some good. As we saw before, some people instinctively know where their natural bent lies, others need guidance. Whatever your case may be, you can determine what you want to do in life by what you like and what you find pleasurable. Do what you like and your talent will shine forth. If a change is suggested, don't hesitate to check it out (most of us have more than one talent). As old Publilius Syrus wrote, "No one knows what he can do till he tries." Get into life, do something, discover what you like and what you can do, and pursue happiness in a line that agrees with your innermost yearnings. Many people may not understand or support you in this endeavor but it doesn't matter: it is your life, it is up to you to decide what goes on in it.

    Find out all you can about how you can perfect your talent (every talent needs some refining) and how you can sell it better to the society and do that. Don't forget your weaknesses. Everyone has lots of them. Acknowledge them but don't worry about them. Improve what you can improve and try to run your life on your strengths, not on your weaknesses.

- Health Management Skills

   You live in your body. Your ability to take good care of your body will determine how well and how long it can serve you. Your personal hygiene, what you eat, your exercise routines and how you manage your emotions will affect your other abilities and your effectiveness in life.

- Money Management Skills

   In a capitalistic society (and most societies are either capitalistic or wishing they were), money is king. Nothing matters half as money. How you manage your money, which is never enough, determines how well you'll fare in the society. Keep a tab on all the money that come into your possession and treat them like precious resources—and they sure are extremely precious. Manage your money with care, caution, thrift and foresight, and it will smoothen and sweeten your life greatly.

- Problem-solving Skills

   Life is always lived forward. In other words, every moment of our forward life is new to us. Problems do arise, sometimes from where we expect them and sometimes from where we least expect them. The secret is not to dodge them but to confront them—and to do so wisely. This is where problem-solving skills come in: sizing up the problem, dividing it into conquerable pieces, mapping out solution strategies, solving it, etc. Problem-solving skills can be developed from experience or through training. However you decide to draw them into your life, do it.

- Risk Management Skills

   As we mentioned above, life is lived forward. That means that there is always a risk factor involved. The trick is not to be afraid of risk but to welcome it as an integral part of your existence. You can't live without it so why not live with it? "Progress," Frederick Wilcox said, "always involves risk; you can't steal second base and keep your foot on first."

A person who risks nothing, does nothing and has nothing. He may be able to avoid suffering and sorrow but he cannot learn, feel, change, grow, love, live. Entering into a relationship of any kind is a risk, doing anything is a risk, even breathing in and out is a risk. Minimize your risks as much as you can but take them.

We all need skills for looking directly into the monstrous face of risks, for minimizing them, and for turning them into the blessings they really are. "Our doubts," Shakespeare wrote in Measure for Measure, "are traitors, and make us lose the good we oft might win, by fearing to attempt."

- **Crisis And Failure Management Skills**

Remember we have not passed this way before, so we are bound to make mistakes and even drive into deep crisis. Crisis and failure, in themselves, do not kill. What kills is what we make of them. Some people have the erroneous view that failure cannot happen to them so when eventually it comes, as it always does, they find it hard to contain. But there is nothing unusual or unnatural about failure. It is part of our experience of consciousness. Never the end of the road as many people make it out to be, it is usually a blessing in disguise. Your ability to manage failure and profit from it will determine how empowered you are to achieve health and happiness.

When failure comes, don't make the mistake of comparing yourself with others. They are living their own lives and you are living yours. Where's the connection?

- **Patience And Perseverance Skills**

    "When nothing seems to help," Jacob Riis wrote, "I go and look at a stonecutter, hammering away at his rock, perhaps a hundred times without as much as a crack showing in it. Yet at the hundred and first blow it will split in two, and I know it was not that blow that did it—but all that had gone before."

    In life we must learn to wait and to keep going despite discouraging circumstances. Expecting to start out on a project or a life course as a winner is often unrealistic and I am constantly surprised by the number and calibre of people I come across who fully expect to always start out on the winning side. Success in handling life issues takes time so that your patience and perseverance are always required.

    "Whatever course you decide upon," Ralph Emerson wrote, "there is always someone to tell you you are wrong. There are always difficulties arising which tempt you to believe that your critics are right. To map out a course of action and follow it to the end, requires some of the same courage which a soldier needs."

(ii) Social Skills

Social skills are those skills we need to function well in the society. Some of these are:

- Communication Skills

    We need to communicate with others either as part of our duties or in the course of our normal daily activities. How well we come across to others determines how well they understand us and how well we achieve the goal of our communication. Being the major route through which we connect to others, communication skills are vitally important for everyone. The better you are at it, the easier your life will be (because other people can decide to make your life a living hell if they don't understand or hate what you are saying—and they will succeed beyond your wildest imagination). A verse in *The Teaching for Merikare* (c. 2135 - 2040 B.C.) said: "Be skillful in speech, that you may be strong; it is the strength of the tongue, and words are braver than all fighting."

• **Listening Skills**

Listening is the other half of communicating. We need to listen to others so that we can understand what they are telling us or their response to our communication. Everybody loves a good listener, so listening skills are very important social skills.

• **Tact**

Life is not a straight line. Sometimes things happen that should not ordinarily have happened. Tact refers to an ability to communicate disagreeable information indirectly and inoffensively.

True, it comes naturally with some personality types and it's strange to others but it is one skill that can make a big difference in a person's social effectiveness, a difference of the order of the difference between night and day. Tact should be learned and consciously put into practice by everyone, especially the introverts to whom it is foreign and despicable.

•**Understanding Nonverbal Clues**

People communicate with words and movements. Participating in a society requires that you learn to understand what people mean by the movements of various parts of their body: body language. Like spoken languages, body language may vary from place to place; certain movements may mean the same thing in all cultures. You must learn to understand and speak the body language used in your society.

- **Self-positioning**
    Self-positioning refers to how you position your unique characteristics to be compatible with and benefit from the social order. Let's say you are artistically inclined. You must learn what society requires from artists like you and comply. How does your particular society expect artists to look? What kind of artistic enterprise is welcomed in the society? What part of this general art world agrees with your person? How do you position yourself in this niche and make the best of it? Which of your personal attributes must you refine and which must you drop or cover? etc.

- **Self-presentation Skills**
    "There needs no ghost, my lord, come from the grave to tell us this" (Shakespeare); that how we present ourselves to the society matters a great deal. In the same book, Hamlet, Shakespeare said: "For the apparel oft proclaims the man." How so true! How we dress, our personal grooming and how we present ourselves to others determine how they react to us. And the voice of the people is the voice of God! If people like you, you have got it made; if you make them dislike or despise you, you are courting disaster of colossal dimensions.
    Present yourself confidently and appear to be who you want people to believe you are. As Daniel Webster wrote, "The world is governed more by appearance than by realities, so that it is fully necessary to seem to know something as it is to know it."

- **Making Friends**

    Most of us cannot survive or find meaningful existence without friends. We must develop skills for winning and keeping friends. While it comes naturally to some of us, some of us must make conscious, consistent efforts to develop skills for winning friends. Learn what you can and let experience help you refine it. Don't be discouraged when you fail. Just keep going. Everybody gets better if they keep at it.

- **Team Playing**

    Many tasks are accomplished by teamwork. As a participant in this concert of life, you must learn skills that allow you to work effectively with others, the gives and the takes, and everything in between. Pay determined attention to this because very few things can be accomplished and enjoyed in this life without teamwork.

(iii) Specialized Skills

Specialized skills are those skills you need to perform your job. A secretary needs communication and typing skills, a professor needs intellectual and research skills, a computer programmer needs programming skills, a technician needs mechanical skills, etc. Your ability to reach the heights at your job will be determined by how much effort you invest into cultivating, perfecting and applying the necessary skills to the relevant tasks.

All the above skills and others we did not consider go into the making of the Skills factor in the ASK MET PF. The more skills you have in the direction being analyzed or evaluated, the greater your empowering unit, other factors being equal.

3. Knowledge

Knowledge, they say, is power. The more you know, the better you can position yourself to handle the issues of life. Consider knowledge like a lever, providing its user with a leverage over the hard nuts of existence. The longer and stronger the lever the easier it is to move mountains of problems. Knowledge is also important for many other reasons:

(i) Problem Identification

Knowledge of a subject (or something related to it) is very useful in the identification of problems in that subject area. How would one know that he has come upon a problem if he does not know anything about the system or how it operates?

(ii) Avoid Waste

There is nothing so wasteful as doing with great efficiency that which doesn't have to be done at all. Knowing what is important and what is trivial, what should be changed and what should be left alone, helps avoid the waste of precious time, energy and resources. It gives the project a focus or handle and leads to a more efficient and profitable use of scarce resources.

(iii) Minimize uncertainty in decision making

Knowing the parameters and dimensions of a problem minimizes the uncertainty in decision making.

(iv) Increase the probability of developing and implementing innovative and effective solutions

Knowledge increases the probability of coming up with breakthrough solutions by providing a firm grip on the problem and the angles of attack from which the problem can be solved.

Great breakthrough solutions come from great ideas and great ideas come from combinations and/or transfers of knowledge.

(v) Take advantage of changing conditions

Things are always changing. Good knowledge of a subject and the conditions around it help people to take advantage of the demands of ever-changing conditions, instead of just coping with them.

(vi) Gives confidence

Knowledge gives confidence. The more you know about a subject, the more ability and confidence to work more constructively and more purposefully you gain.

(vii) A foundation for future progress

Nothing is created out of a vacuum. All human progress, be it scientific, social or personal, is built upon previous knowledge. The most progressive nations, Ralph Emerson observed, are those that navigate the most.

In summary, knowledge is an essential tool in the toolbox of life. Without it you are handicapped in a major way and you cannot handle some problems that life is sure to serve you. No wonder Aristotle said that "educated men are as much superior to uneducated men as the living are to the dead." Living souls (educated men and women in Aristotle's model) can handle problems on their own, dead people (uneducated men and women) need the living to determine their destiny.

Gain as much knowledge as you can about every subject that interests you. Knowledge is always valuable. You never know when you may need it.

As Pascal said, "Knowledge is like a sphere in space; the greater its volume, the larger its contact with the unknown."

The more you know, the greater control you gain over the reality of your existence.

There are about three ways we gain knowledge:
    (a) From what we soak up from our surroundings,
    (b) From what we are forced to learn, and
    (c) From what we draw into ourselves by our own volition.

(a) What we soak up from our surroundings

The place you live, work or play affects how much you know. If you were born into an investor family, for example, you would learn a lot about interest rates, government monetary regulations, money markets, stock markets, etc. without being formally taught. You soak them up by being exposed to them in your daily conversations and family life. They become second nature to you almost automatically. Should you decide to make your living in financial services, your family background would give you a distinct advantage.

(b) What we are forced to learn

A vast majority of mankind don't want to learn. They would do anything to avoid drawing knowledge into their brains. That's why there is formal education. In a formal educational setting, there is a curriculum of study, a list of courses the student is expected to study and pass.

Like most human beings, students always resist learning and it is the job of teachers and educators to make them learn what they are supposed to learn. Sometimes the mere threat of a hard life ahead without formal education is enough to convince students to learn. In some other situations other incentives and even the threat of force or denial of privileges are necessary to force students to gain knowledge. A small group of students love learning for its own sake.

Needless to say, education or knowledge received in this way is easily forgotten or dropped from the brain once the formal education is completed (except if it is necessary for an immediate task or job). For all its deficiencies, formal education remains our best chance of transmitting knowledge to a large proportion of the population.

Most professions where you require a license to practice demand that you study and pass a set of courses. A good incentive for formal education, don't you think? You may not be keen on advanced calculus but you must study and pass it if you want to fulfil your dreams of becoming an engineer, for example.

(c) What we draw into ourselves by our own volition

The knowledge we gain by our own volition is the most influential, powerful and durable portion of our total store of knowledge. As we mentioned earlier, drawing in knowledge comes easier to some personality types than to others. To anyone who pulls in knowledge into himself there is a reward, a huge reward. The reward? Mastery. The power to master situations, to generate great ideas and the power to achieve great results. Knowledge is power and it is most powerful when it is enthusiastically sought for and welcomed with open arms and gratitude. It performs more of its magic when it flows downstream into a willing, ready and respecting receptacle than when it is forced upstream into a flat surface where it is nothing but a necessary nuisance.

Develop a taste and a longing for knowledge for its own sake and it will increase your power and influence over reality beyond what you might imagine possible. The more you know, the easier it is to confront and overcome challenges.

The more knowledge you have in the direction being analyzed, the greater your empowering unit, every other factor in the ASK MET PF being equal.

4. Money

"Money," Sir Edmund Stockdale wrote, "isn't everything—but it's a long way ahead of what comes next." There are several reasons why money is such a precious asset in capitalistic societies. Some of these reasons are:
      (i) It is a great facilitator
      (ii) It is the most powerful language on earth
      (iii) It is a bulwark against vicissitudes
      (iv) It provides a bridge to others
      (v) It gives social standing
      (vi) It is a great sanctifier and justifier

(i) A great facilitator

Somerset Maugham said: "Money is like a sixth sense without which you cannot make a complete use of the other five."

In a capitalistic society, money is the great facilitator of life. With money in your pocket, you can choose to satisfy your senses of sight, hearing, taste, smell and touch. Without money, you have no choice but to accept whatever happens.

If you desire a beautiful girl, for example, you would have to pray and wish that something extraordinary happens to force her into your arms—and at the rate miracles happen in real life, you may have to wait until after your death. If, on the other hand, you are very rich, beautiful girls will flock to you as bees converge on a lump of honey. Your problem will be determining which one of them to choose. Money is a great facilitator not only in the area of romance but in all aspects of life in a capitalistic environment. It opens doors, smoothens roads and makes the achievement of your goal easier and less painful.

(ii) The most powerful language on earth

If you can speak *money-talk* fluently you will be understood wherever man is found. As Alfred Behan said, "Money speaks sense in a language all nations understand."

Language is a tool to communicate with others and make them respond to you. Nothing elicits support and action from other people like money. You can spend years trying to sell someone on the benefits of allowing you to use a piece of his property to build a school to serve the needs of the children in your community without success but when you offer him a large sum of money in exchange for the property he will begin to understand that your idea is a noble one.

As a language, money provides individuals in a capitalistic society access to the goods and services produced and promoted by others. It is very hard for a food vendor, for example, to understand that you are hungry if you don't speak the appropriate *money-talk* or its equivalent. "When I was young," Oscar Wilde wrote, "I used to think that money was the most important thing in life; now that I am old, I know it is."

(iii) A bulwark against vicissitudes

When hard times come, as they always do, the rich man can fall on his reserves or the money in the bank. A poor man, struggling to make ends meet, lacks such a safeguard and is bound to be adversely battered by economic recessions and reversals. In other words, the poor man is at the mercy of his environment while the rich man can successfully ride the ups and downs of life. Being the owner of the means of production he can decide to cut the size and salary of his workforce, increase the prices of his goods and services, lobby the government to come to his rescue, sell some of his assets, dip into his savings or move to a better country or place. His friends or other captains of industry can also help him out for, as Charles Dickens wrote, "money and goods are certainly the best of references." A poor man visited by the same calamity runs the risk of losing everything he claims title to, his family and all his friends—no one in his senses wants to be associated with a drowning man.

(iv) A bridge to others

As we discussed before, we all need others in our lives. We can win friends by our charm, good behavior and social skills but nothing works like money. When all else fails, money always emerges triumphant. What an influence money exerts on the human mind! "Money," Henry Fielding said, "will say more in one moment than the most eloquent lover can in years." The reason why money is so powerful in relationships is that it is such a consensus builder; there is nothing we all agree upon like money. As Voltaire said, "When it is a question of money, everybody is of the same religion."

People like money because of its great power in the community of men. If you have money they will love you too. Well, not you exactly but you plus your money. When your well dries up they'll all flee.

(v) Social standing

Nicolas Boileau-Despreaux is quoted to have said: "Money gives appearance of beauty even to ugliness, but everything becomes frightful with poverty."

Money does make you look good in the public eye. In other words, it improves your social standing. People respond differently to you and your opinions all of a sudden begin to carry enormous weight. Just saying hello to someone is enough to make a news headline. Before you arrived at your glorious success, people had written you off as a babbler and a never-do-well, now the words that fall from your mouth are as precious as pure gold. When you were poor or nondescript, no one seemed to know that you existed. Now everyone claims you are their good friend and everyone invites you to weddings, parties, and other special events. You are now a genius, an illustrious son of the community, a very wonderful person, a role model whose biography is sought after and copied as if it is a script written by the finger of God. What a wonderful change money brings!

(vi) A great sanctifier and justifier

Nothing covers sins and justifies bad behavior like money. "Success," George Bernard Shaw said, "covers a multitude of blunders." He also said: "Make money, and the whole nation will conspire to call you a gentleman." Psychologists (usually the quacks, of course) would hurry to recommend your habits to the rest of the population as the essence of excellence.

The standards are different for the rich man than for the poor man, despite all pretensions to the contrary. "The world tolerates conceit from those who are successful, but not from anybody else," John Blake observed and T.E. Brown wrote: "Money is honey, my little sonny, and a rich man's joke is always funny."

The amount of money you have access to in the direction being evaluated determines the size of your empowering unit, every other thing being equal. Some say that money is not

always important. That may be true but it is hard to imagine real life situations where having money is a disadvantage.
Poverty leads to a diminution of your empowering unit. You cannot always choose what you want to do and how you want others to perceive you. This reduces the size of your empowering unit and may make you feel helpless, worthless, powerless and hopeless.

5. Equipment

In many cases equipment and money go together but there are instances where equipment stands as a parameter in its own right. For example, a researcher may not have money but if he has access to the equipment he needs his empowering unit is broadened. A research scientist with access to sophisticated and technologically advanced equipment is more empowered than one with only crude, unreliable equipment.

6. Time

> *You wake up in the morning, and lo! your purse is magically filled with twenty-four hours of the unmanufactured tissue of the universe of your life. It is yours. It is the most precious of possessions. No one can take it from you. It is unstealable. And no one receives either more or less than you receive.*
>
> Arnold Bennett

How much of this "unmanufactured tissue of the universe of your life" you invest or employ in the direction being analyzed determines the size and strength of your empowering unit. You may be potentially the most creative mind that has ever graced the surface of the earth but if you spend most of your time watching television and little or no time on creative pursuits, you will never fulfil the promise of your creativity. If on the other hand, you are moderately gifted in creativity but you spend a lot of time developing and utilizing your creative side, you may end up being the actual most creative mind in history.

"You cannot kill time," Henry David Thoreau wrote, "without injuring eternity." You cannot kill time without reducing your power to perform. There is very little you can do without spending time on it.

Most of the time it is our indiscipline or laziness that prevents us from investing enough time in our dreams. Sometimes relationships, family responsibilities and administrative duties over and above our normal hours of work eat up our time.

At other times it is poverty or lack of money that pulls us back. Imagine that you are struggling to pay your rent and put food on the table by working two jobs, how much time can you have for the pursuit of progress? But some great souls are able to overcome even this handicap. They reduce their expenses in all ways possible and work only few hours on outside jobs to meet their remaining basic needs and invest the rest of their time on projects that are important for their self-actualization.

Risky and hard? Yes, but, as Herodotus said, "great deeds are usually wrought at great risks." A price has to be paid for progress. As James Cook said, "Life is going to dole out a share of pain to you no matter where you hide," so why not live daringly, boldly and fearlessly; taste the relish to be found in putting forth the best within you, of fulfilling your heart desires.

7. People

As we saw when we discussed the need for others, other people are very important for our happiness and progress. People are important as a factor in our empowering unit in two major ways:

        (i) As a connection to the rest of society
        (ii) As a source of empowerment

(i) A connection to the rest of society

You, as an individual, can only be at one place at a time. Yet several other things that are important to you are happening in other places and areas of the society. How can you remain where you are and pursue your interests in other areas? Connections, that's how. You need people who are in those places to help you out. You need to cultivate cordial relationships with such people and show them that it is in their own best interests to help you. For example, if you are looking for a job, a friend you have helped out in the past may be able to connect you to the job you need. Having that friend increased your empowering unit as far as finding that job was concerned. Being a friend or relative of a person of high social standing can also do wonders for you. Make no mistake about it: people love people who have "good connections" to the powers that be. In competitive societies, who you know is often more important than what you know, what you can do or who you are.

(ii) A source of empowerment

People are also important to you as a source of empowerment. Most projects you undertake demand more talents than you have for its successful completion. You need people with such other talents to supplement your own empowering unit with parts of their own. For example, imagine that you are a writer. You have very good writing skills. You plan to write a book that will use illustrations but you are neither artistically inclined nor gifted. You need to find an artist to help you out. The artist would be supplementing your empowering unit with a part of his. You also need to sell your work to a publisher or buyer but you are either not a good salesperson or not interested in executing that aspect of your project. You need to find a salesperson to supplement your empowering unit with his; etc.

A word of caution: While people are important for our happiness and progress, this does not mean that we should turn over our lives to others to live for us. As we have stressed several times in this book, our lives are ours to live; no one will live it for us. People may help us out in mutually supportive alliances as we have seen above but "no one is great enough or wise enough for any of us to surrender our destiny to" (Henry Miller). As Lord Halifax said, "A man is to go about his business as if he had not a friend in the world to help him in it." Get all the help you can get but please live your life yourself.

8. Social Fund

Social fund in this model refers to how the society in general perceives you and how far it is willing to support or patronize you and your idea/project. As we discussed under attitude above, people perceive and evaluate you based on some social identity categories. These identity elements determine, to a large extent, how much societal goodwill you have—and societal goodwill is so important to you because you cannot live without or outside the society. We shall consider three categories of social fund:

(i) Your physical beauty
(ii) Social fund connected with your social identity
  • Race, tribe or group
  • Sex (gender)
  • Social class
(iii) Social fund connected with your work
  • Novelty
  • Demand
  • Status

(i) Physical beauty

How you look has a tremendous effect on how people perceive you and how they treat you. People love beautiful people and hate to be associated with anyone who does not look good. Beauty is a social fund and like money
  • is a great facilitator,
  • is a bulwark against adversity,
  • provides a bridge to others,
  • gives social standing, and
  • is a great sanctifier and justifier

Beauty, when wisely used like money, is a great facilitator in human affairs. It can open doors for you where otherwise there would be none. It smoothens your way, giving you the ability to slide into good situations and slide out of unfavorable circumstances. It pays to be beautiful.

It can also act as a bulwark against adversity for you. When you are in trouble it is relatively very easy for people to run to your rescue. People love to help (and brag about helping) beautiful people caught in the web of adversity. They hope that by so doing their social fund will rub off on them or that the beautiful person will become their friend, which is a highly priced social asset. It would be difficult to find someone willing to help an ugly person in the same situation, because they cannot see any benefit in doing so.

Beauty, as everyone knows, provides a bridge to others. Everybody loves to deal with beautiful people but no one wants to be caught dead dealing with a sack of drooping flesh. As Aronson (1984) found: "When seen in the company of a beautiful woman, a man is perceived differently from when he is seen with an unattractive woman" (p.298). Beauty draws others to you like a magnet draws iron to itself. With beauty in your skin, your need for others is taken care of automatically, if you play your other cards well.

Being attractive also gives you social standing. Your ideas and opinions are more important with beauty than without. Aronson (1984) also found that "attractive women have more impact on men than less attractive women" (p. 297)—their wishes and opinions are respected more. When there is a dispute as to who should get what and who shouldn't, like a job for example, people tend to favour the more beautiful person (Aronson 1984, p. 298).

Beauty, like money, is also a great sanctifier and justifier in the public's eye. "It seems attractive people are given the benefit of the doubt. Their desirable actions are attributed to them, but their undesirable actions are attributed to the effects of the situation, other people, or an unfortunate accident" (Aronson 1984, p. 297). You can get away with more if you are beautiful than if you are not.

(ii) Social fund connected with your social identity

(a) Race, tribe or group

If your race, tribe or group is the one favoured by the society, you have a high social fund (something like more money in your pocket) and if your race, tribe or group is despised or hated by the society, you have a low social fund (i.e. it will subtract from or make ineffective some or all of your empowering unit).

You cannot be as strong in places where you have a low social fund as you can be where you are welcomed and evaluated for who you are. All your good qualities and abilities will be negated to some degree by a low social fund which may in turn affect your ability to perform. Whether you like it or not and no matter what you do, a low social fund connected with your social identity will affect you in one way or another. Your best bet is to acknowledge it and try to work around it. Do not compare yourself with a colleague from a more favored group (your circumstances are different); do your best with what you have in areas that are open to you.

A low social fund due to your race or group may make you feel helpless, worthless, powerless and hopeless and raise your need to be dependent on others but you shouldn't let it bring you that low. As we said before, your life is yours to live, so you have choices. You can find ways to shore up your self-esteem and to affirm your right to a meaningful existence which nature bestowed on you by giving you the privilege of life. What you make of your social fund is up to you!

(b) Sex (gender)

In most societies, as far as this author knows, men and women are not treated equally. Very often, women have a lower social fund relative to men. This low social fund could cause women to feel helpless (as we saw above in connection with race) and heighten their need for dependence on others and their conformity to norms. But women are fighting back and are, thus far, succeeding.

Gender also affects what society expects of us. Men are expected to succeed and when they don't, society bills them for their failure in pounds of flesh. They may even lose their families and their friends because of that. Women are not expected to succeed so if they fail in any enterprise they suffer no devastating social consequences. In other words, failure can decrease or wipe out the ingredients of a man's empowering unit (through a sharp decline in his social fund) but it may not affect a woman under similar conditions. This too is changing.

(c) Social Class

Like money, a high social class comes with a high social fund. Your choices are broader and your life and opportunities in the society are less restricted. You can choose to obtain or pursue any skill, knowledge or advantage you want. You are the darling of the society. People love to associate with you and be nice to you. A low social class (usually socioeconomic), due to poverty especially, reduces your empowering unit and makes your life more insecure and dependent on others. Your choices are fewer and more out of reach. Everyone makes an effort to avoid you and you are treated as the scum of the earth, without respect or consideration. This author has never seen or heard of a society where poor people are not despised.

(iii) Social fund connected with your work

Whether people like or dislike what you are doing determines how they react to you and treat you. Here we shall discuss three aspects of work that affect your social fund in relation to your work or profession.

(a) Novelty

Being naturally insecure, people hate new things—until they become accepted by the general public. As Denise Shekerjian wrote, "New things put a tremendous strain on old opinions. People are slow to change; the resistance to throwing

The Empowering Unit 151

out one's entire stock of old opinions is iron strong" (Shekerjian 1990, p.56). This resistance to novelty differs from place to place and from time to time. During war times or chaotic periods, for example, people become less resistant to change than during stable times. In any case, innovations or new ideas are always greeted with skepticism and sometimes with hostility. The social fund connected with your new idea will determine how and when it (and by association, you) succeeds.

(b) Demand

A medical doctor has a higher social fund than a fast-talking salesman. His services are demanded and appreciated while the salesman is perceived as a crook who is exploiting people's insecurities and weaknesses for his personal gain. We may not agree with that but that's the verdict of the almighty society. So if there is a high demand and respectability for your work, people will look favorably on you—increasing your empowering unit, should you decide to exploit that aspect of your reality. If you are doing something that no one needs or that is ahead of its time, society will not empower you with her support.

(c) Status

A university professor has more social status than a roadside mechanic, even though the mechanic may be making more money than the professor.

The status of the place you work also affects your social fund and impact on the society. If you are a professor at Harvard University you will be respected and patronized more (in fact your research papers will be more influential) than if you are doing the same research as a professor at Harvey University. One is socially empowered, the other rides on deflated tires.

Chapter Fourteen

The Motivation Vector

The motivation vector, V_m, we saw, is given as

$$V_m = V/V_t$$

We saw that it is the intensity of the motivation driving the individual in the direction of the force. It is a ratio of the motivation velocity the individual is exposed to, V, to his or her responsiveness, V_t.

High sphericity individuals respond more to the same V than low sphericity individuals because their V_t is lower (V must be in the same direction of interest to all the particles being compared). We also saw that for the same V, one particle may be twice as motivated as another particle indicating that human biological nature play a big role in the individual's motivational characteristics.

The motivation to achieve is one motivation that runs across every segment of the population in a competitive society. We shall use it here to explain what V_m is all about with respect to this theory.

What Motivates People to Achieve?

First we must ask: what motivates people to achieve? Are human beings born with a motivation to achieve? What pushes people to achieve?

If you have been following this theory from the beginning, you know what our answer will be: INSECURITY. Insecurity is what motivates human beings to achieve.

The motivation to achieve is a behavioral characteristic of human beings like any other. In other words it is a form of motion like every other human behavior we discussed in the preceding chapters. It too is driven by insecurity or lack of it.

What Produces Insecurity With Respect to Achievement Motivation?

In the case of general life on earth, we saw that insecurity is produced by our inadequacy to control the issues of life to our satisfaction—an inadequacy which leads to a potential difference between what we want and what we feel we can get. This results, as we discussed, in a need for self-defense, a desire to avoid reality, a need for others, a need to be greater than others, and a need for emotional expression.

In a similar way, achievement motivation-producing insecurity is produced by the potential difference between what we want and what we feel we can get especially in a competitive society. We emphasize competitive society here because personal achievement, in its common usage, is a feature of the competitive society and has little or no meaning in non-competitive environments. In fact, φ_p is essentially meaningless in non-competitive societies, assuming such societies exist.

In a very competitive environment, there are no guarantees, no safe havens, no safe positions. Everything is up for grabs. You may have something now and in a few moments it moves into the possession of another person. So there is a constant struggle to maintain your grounds (what you already have) while stretching out to gain new territories because you never know what is going to happen to what you have now. Someone may be harboring a secret plan to unseat you and you need alternative plans should his bid succeed.

This chaotic, tumultuous situation fostered by competition produces potential differences (between what you want and what you are certain you are able to get) which generate insecurity. It is this insecurity that motivates you to achieve. Competition crystallizes achievement motivation like nothing else. As we saw when we discussed the need to be greater than others in chapter 8, if you could have anything you desired and no one could add or subtract anything from you, you will be fully secure and you will not be motivated to achieve anything. The more socially insecure you feel, the more you want to achieve and get the society on your side.

As we saw in earlier chapters, insecurity is the root of selfishness—which, in turn, is the root of man's inhumanity to man. Since competition produces insecurity, a very competitive society is a selfish society. The banner of such societies is: "Everyone for himself and the Devil take the hindmost." All the traits we saw connected with natural insecurity become even more pronounced with high levels of competition. Lying and falsehood, cunningness and wickedness become the pillars of the state. The ability to pull others down and elevate oneself becomes a precious and praise-worthy virtue. It becomes very hard to get ahead in life without good measures of selfishness, brutality, dishonesty and crookedness because these are the natural products of large quantities of insecurity. The most aggressive and ruthless move to positions of power and influence. The road to success becomes paved with double-dealing and inhumanity. Evil people prosper and the righteous suffer. Seething rivalries lead to emotional breakdowns and bitter defeats.

Despite all its drawbacks, competition, when properly managed, is a good thing. This author cannot imagine human progress without competition. True, high levels of competition among human beings produce floods of insecurity but insecurity is not foreign to the human condition, as we saw before. Our inadequacy is a given. The only problem here is that we are not all equally inadequate; some are more insecure than others. The more insecure (and hence more selfish) among us will naturally do better than the less selfish in a competitive society. In other words, the less selfish, the less wicked, the less dishonest, and the less aggressive individuals will suffer more frustrations and failures than the rest of us. High sphericity individuals must cultivate selfishness in order to succeed in such societies. Righteousness cannot co-exist with torrents of competition and insecurity without persecution and anguish.

Competition sets things in motion. A competitive society is a dynamic society. And dynamism leads to creativity, improved skills, progress and prosperity. Aspirations soar, people dare to hope for and pursue great things, people discover hidden gifts or talents they did not know they had and human beings achieve great heights. Notice that every emergency, every crisis (all insecurity-producing situations) reveals unsuspected resources and talents in some people and rouses heightened motivation in almost all of us. Competition produces a strengthening of character. For as fire tempers iron, hardships toughen character—and hardships, uncertainties, barriers and hurdles are constant features of highly competitive societies.

Since Abundance Reduces Insecurity, Does It Destroy Achievement Ability?

Abundance may dull the edge of achievement motivation by reducing insecurity (i.e. by increasing φ_p) but it doesn't reduce achievement ability. In fact, it makes possible the nourishing of talent or the increase in the size of the individual's empowering unit, d_e, on a scale which would otherwise be impossible.

Achievement ability is a function of φ_p, not V_m. In other words, high levels of motivation do not necessarily translate into high achievement. You may be highly motivated to build a great business, for example, but if you do not have the necessary start-up capital (and enough reserves to keep you going until people discover you), the relevant skills or experience and the requisite social fund, you simply won't realize your dreams. Achievement is a function of your operating momentum, φ_p, not just your motivation, V_m.

We did hundreds of experiments in our laboratory with particles as depicted in Figure 12.1 and found that φ_p, not V_m, determines how far the outside particle (the individual) penetrates into the large tank (society).

φ_p, we saw, is a product of d_e and V_m. Abundance does decrease V_m (which is a function of insecurity) but it increases d_e which is often a larger proportion of φ_p than raw V_m. Therefore, abundance increases achievement. The more you have, the more you can get.

How does abundance increase the size of the empowering unit, d_e? Improved self-esteem (attitude), greater access to needed skills and knowledge, more money and better equipment, more free time to pursue goals (you are not busy worrying about where your next meal will come from), greater ability to employ or exploit superior people and a much better social goodwill. How much better can it get?

How does abundance reduce V_m? By reducing the pinching feelings of insecurity (the potential difference between what you want and what you feel you can get decreases). You are making a good living and you have most of the things you need to make your life comfortable. There is no fear that this situation will change drastically in the foreseeable future. The pulverizing pressures of poverty and social rejection are foreign news to you. You are more or less secure in your world. Why would you spend sleepless nights plotting strategies to achieve?

Notice that immigrants seeking wealth are always more motivated to achieve than indigenes. For one thing, their place in the society and their social fund are tenuous at best. This insecurity drives them to take up jobs most natives find beneath them. It also drives the more able among them to take the necessary risks to achieve new heights. Their activities plus the society's general competitiveness cause ripples in the security of the natives, leading some of the indigenes to greater motivations and others to hate and envy. Without insecurity there would be no motivation to achieve. Without hunger there would be no need to eat.

Different Directions For Achievement

As we have seen, insecurity affects behavior differently depending on the λ_p. In the same way people are motivated to achieve different goals based on their λ_p. Lower λ_p individuals or people with smaller empowering units, d_e, tend to be driven by insecurity to achieve goals that are more personal:

(i) Personal wealth—to escape poverty and the terrible things that come with it
(ii) Recognition—a desire to be known, appreciated and respected
(iii) Personal power—to widen one's sphere of influence, to be greater than someone

Higher λ_p individuals or people with larger empowering units, d_e, can afford to be driven by global or less self-oriented concerns (i.e. by insecurity outside of themselves):
(i) The challenge of an unexplained mystery
(ii) The welfare of others
(iii) Making the world a better place for everyone

Does this mean that somebody's life work is an indication of his sphericity? Sometimes, not always. Some people pursue the welfare of others not because they are selfless but as a means of winning praise, recognition, fame or fortune (all selfish ends); others (extremely few) do so out of a selfless devotion to humanity.

Please note that the distinction we made above does not imply that lower λ_p persons have small d_e and higher λ_p individuals have large d_e. What we are saying is that low λ_p and small d_e (more insecure) or high λ_p and large d_e (less insecure) tend to act alike. Behavior is driven by insecurity once again.

As our working formula above shows, where higher λ_p persons are involved, they will be practically more motivated than lower λ_p individuals given the same V because of their lower V_t. In other words, given equal motivation the higher λ_p person shows a higher level of aspiration than a lower λ_p individual.

Chapter Fifteen

φ_p and Insecurity

The comparison of individuals based on their φ_p is done by scoring each individual's d_e (ASK MET PF) and V_m (V/V_t) for the situation desired.

As you must have noticed from our discussion of the various factors involved in determining φ_p, a low φ_p signifies a low social standing which translates into a high social insecurity, and a high φ_p means a high social standing or low social insecurity. Social insecurity refers to a feeling that one is not what or who one desires to be in the society.

High social insecurity aggravates our natural feelings of insecurity while a low or minimal social insecurity may not. For example, if someone's level of security is 0.70, a high social insecurity may make it feel like 0.5 or even less. Since human psychological behavior is related to human insecurity (this is the cornerstone of our theory, you remember), an exasperation of a person's feeling of insecurity will make him behave like someone with a lower λ_p. This being the case you will find low λ_p behavior more predominant among downtrodden people than among the favored classes. Stealing, alcoholism, addiction to drugs, promiscuity, wickedness, violent aggression as well as more religious fervor, more dependence on others (experts, gurus, psychics, etc.) and more conformity to social norms.

The need for protection from a hostile world (selfishness, hate, vindictiveness); the need to escape reality (a feeling of helplessness; recklessness; laziness; dependence on others or God); a narrow world view; the need for others (desire to be loved, accepted and cherished); the need to be greater than others (wickedness, aggression towards "weaker" people); emotional instability; and dynamic practicality (aversion to risk, inability to persevere or persist) will be higher, relatively speaking, in people with low φ_p than high φ_p individuals. These traits associated with insecurity have already been discussed in connection with λ_p. They apply here as well.

Everyone's insecurity does not, however, respond equally to aggravation by social insecurity. Higher λ_p individuals maintain their ground better than low λ_p persons (see Figure 15.1). Remember we saw that high λ_p persons do not respond very well to social processing. This is what is happening here.

The insecurity of very low λ_p individuals may be exasperated by low φ_p to the point where their personal and social functioning are impaired. They may withdraw totally to their own worlds and indulge in delusions, hallucinations and bizarre, dangerous behavior. This kind of total breakdown of the functional center of personality will be extremely rare in people with high φ_p (the upper class of the society) who are not subject to the crushing pressures of low φ_p.

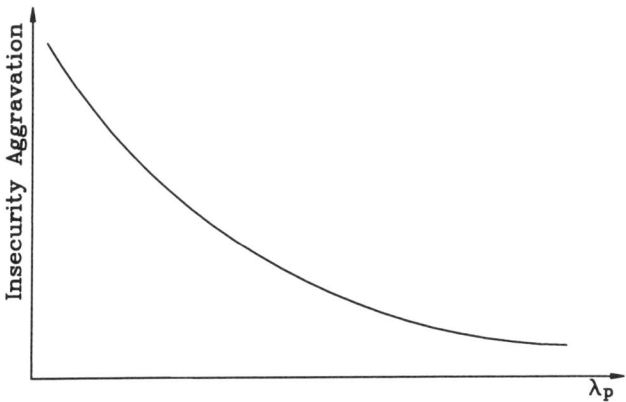

Figure 15.1. Aggravation of insecurity by low φ_p.

High φ_p "dresses up" individual behavior instead of aggravating it. People who have experienced some kind of personal development, thereby increasing their φ_p, and those born into high φ_p are more secure than people with equal λ_p but lower φ_p. Their φ_p dresses up their behavior even though their λ_p remains the same.

But high φ_p does not dress up everyone equally. Lower λ_p persons are dressed up more than high λ_p individuals (see Figure 15.2). Their (low λ_p individuals) behavior is so dressed up by their high φ_p that they appear as naturally high λ_p individuals but inwardly their low λ_p behavior is waiting to be kindled.

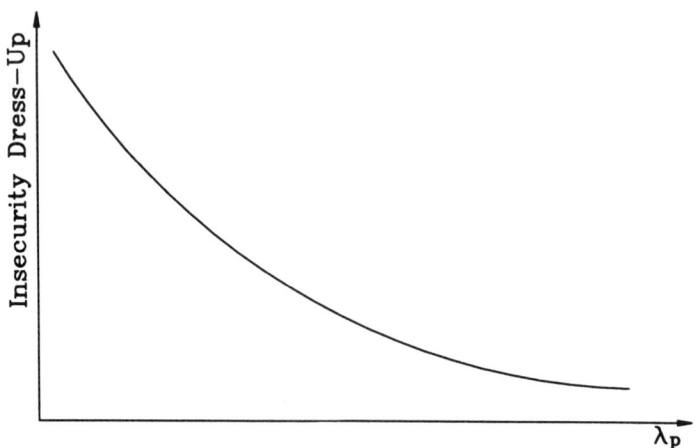

Figure 15.2. "Dress up" of insecurity by high φ_p.

A friend of this author suggested that people may also be divided into eight groups based on their φ_p, as with λ_p, as follows (see Figure 15.3):

Group	Characteristic
1	Bitter, Withdraw to self
2	Helpless, Give Up, While time away
3	Reckless, Go against the law
4	Drift, Take whatever comes and don't complain
5	Plod, Work hard to be accepted
6	Push, Struggle to the top
7	Win, Strive to settle at the top
8	Maintain, Settle at the top

φ_p **and Insecurity** 165

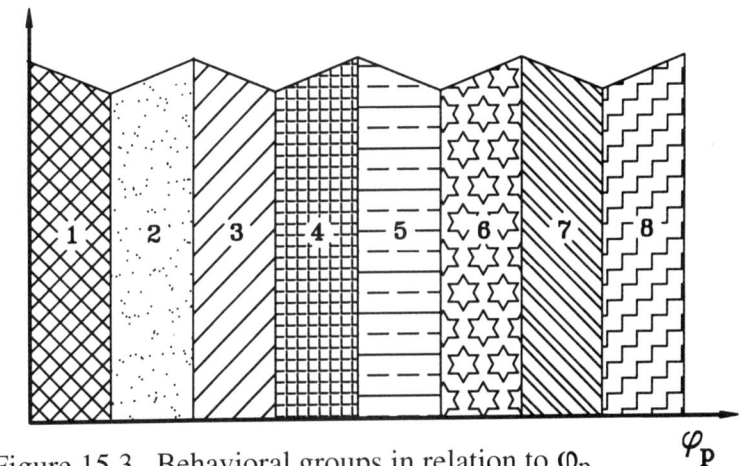

Figure 15.3. Behavioral groups in relation to φ_p.

You may have observed that people of the same trade or profession tend to behave alike. This is not always because people with the same nature gravitate to the same profession; their behaviors are similar because their φ_p (especially their skills and outlook on life or self-esteem) are similar because of their work. Their social insecurity levels are similar so their social behaviors are similar. For example, Yount (1986) found that male and female coal miners describe themselves with the same masculine-type adjectives while male and female caregivers describe themselves with the same feminine-type adjectives. If these people are however studied more closely it will be found that their λ_p are different.

You may also have seen that people from the same country (or the same section of the country) tend to behave alike. If you have not travelled widely or had experience with various people from different cultures, you will be tempted to believe that the personalities of all the people from a particular place are all the same. And you will be wrong. People from the same place have similar behaviors because many elements of their φ_p are similar relative to other groups—their attitudes to life, what they consider important in life, their life skills and other skills, and their experiences in life tend to be similar. If you study them individually, however, you will discover that they are all different from each other, just like people in your own society.

In your own country, you can see the differences in the behavior of individuals readily (though an outsider thinks all of you behave the same way). This is because you are able to hold φ_p constant to a certain degree so that λ_p is projected on your screen (though fuzzily, partly because φ_p is not completely constant in your model).

Implications of All These

Now, let's briefly consider the implications of our portrait in such areas as research, behavioral change and reform, personal performance and achievement, relationships and social justice.

Research

What we learn from all these is that human insecurity and thus behavior, springs from two sources: nature and environment. The environment is obviously not as strong as nature in determining human behavior but its effects are significant enough to be taken into serious consideration. φ_p (the environmental factor) is subject to change but λ_p (the biological factor) cannot be changed once it is formed in the womb.

So, in order to study and categorize human biologically-based psychological behavior (λ_p), φ_p must be kept reasonably constant and to study the effect of the environment (φ_p), λ_p must be kept reasonably constant, if reliable results are to be obtained. Many problems in human personality understanding will be quickly resolved if this is done. Without keeping these separate, a good portrait of human behavior cannot be obtained.

Behavioral Change and Reform

As far as this author can see at this moment, λ_p cannot be changed. All efforts for reforming or improving human behavior should be directed to changing the elements of φ_p—improving general attitude to life and self-esteem, increasing the store of knowledge, imparting empowering skills and knowledge, reducing social inequalities, etc. A significant change in φ_p will result in a significant change in behavior, especially among individuals in the lower classes of society whose φ_p are desperately low. This behavioral change is subject to reversals but it can be brought right back up and maintained with a good management strategy.

Personal Performance and Achievement

(i) Get closer to your λ_p domain

You will perform better and be happier working in areas that agree with your inner longings. Don't waste your time in jobs that are at variance with your λ_p. There is nothing wrong with your λ_p. Don't try to be someone else. Be yourself and enjoy it.

(ii) Increase the size of your empowering unit, d_e

Your empowering unit consists of your attitude to life (your self-esteem), the skills you have developed, the knowledge you have drawn into yourself, the amount of money you have access to, equipment that is available to you, the time you have to work on your dreams, the people who may be able to help you, and the goodwill of the society that goes with you. Most of these components of your d_e can be improved if you put your mind to it. Try to increase as many of these resources as you can. Use a log book to record your personal empowerment improvement activities, the progress you have made and the areas that need to be worked on.

(iii) Work yourself into 'hot' desire

Increase your V_m by doing your best to feel, in your mind, all the insecurities that are closing in on your soul and what life would be without them. Think of all the money and all the attention you will get from the rest of the society if you achieve glorious results in your life. Now, go for it.

Relationships

(i) Match λ_p and φ_p as closely as you can

You are better off, in this author's opinion, with someone who thinks and acts like you—someone who speaks the same behavioral language as you do, someone who does not find your lifestyle offensive.

Opposites do attract but it is always better and safer for birds of the same feathers to flock together. Someone's special talents or attributes may complement yours but can you live with the rest of the package? He may be very romantic and charming but can you live with his criminal and unstable nature? He may be a genius and very famous but can you live with his boring, all-work-and-no-play orientation to life? She may be very beautiful and you will look good with her on your side but can you live with her temper tantrums?

(ii) λ_p is more critical than ϕ_p

Biological nature is more critical in the choice of your partner than environmental or social factors. The environmental factor (ϕ_p) can be changed but biological nature (λ_p) is very difficult, if not impossible, to change. Someone from a different background, a different culture or a different race can pick up attitudes, skills and other components of his partner's environment and adjust to meet them; biological nature does not yield to adjustments. It (biology) can sometimes be controlled with drugs but drugs have not yet been developed to cover all aspects of human behavior—and never will be.

(iii) If you are already in a relationship

Make an effort to understand and adjust to your partner's λ_p and ϕ_p, if it is at all possible. As we stressed before, for our happiness, nothing is as important as our relationships. If you can put in all those hours at work and strive to improve your work skills as you do, you sure can invest more time and effort in your relationship which is far more important for your health and happiness than your work.

Treating People

More insecure people (low λ_p and ϕ_p) are, relatively, more unreliable and shifty. They respond better to harsh, strict treatment or intimidation. Never be too gentle or kind to them (they love to be subdued, despite their outward suggestions to the contrary). They regard kindness an indication of weakness. They respect people who are harsh, "strong" and assertive. Intimidation works like magic in competitive situations.

Less insecure people (high λ_p and ϕ_p) are less shifty or more stable. Treat them kindly and respectfully. You lose them if you try to openly assert some "power" over them.

Social Justice and Engineering

(i) A classless, crime-free society is an impossible ideal
Human beings are naturally insecure in the world. Their behavior is driven and conditioned by their insecurities. It is not possible to design a society where the manifestations of these powerful determinants of behavior are totally absent. A classless, crime-free society is therefore an impossible ideal. Insecurity will always cause people to seek to be greater than the next person so that class will always be an ever-present social identity element. Crime too can never be abolished from human societies but it can be reduced if the sources of insecurity in the society are reduced.

(ii) Reducing social inequality and insecurity
Leaders of society can reduce social inequalities and insecurities by working hard to change detrimental societal attitudes, by giving everyone equal access to knowledge, skills, and jobs, and by eliminating prejudice in all its forms. This of course will be hard to come by in democratic societies because politicians naturally pitch one group against the other to win votes—the old divide-and-conquer technique that has refused to die.

In another book, this author demonstrates that the fact that we are an insecure and evil race does not mean that we cannot design and run a good society where everyone's needs are practically (not ideally) met and the promise of life is realized. By means of insights gained through particle physics, he sets forth how we can minimize our collective insecurity and maximize our happiness without limiting our progress.

References

Aronson, E. 1984. *The Social Animal*. Fourth edition. New York: W.H. Freeman and Company.

Carver, C.S. & Scheier, M.F. 1988. *Perspectives on Personality*. Needham Heights, Mass.: Allyn and Bacon, Inc.

Faris, R.E.L. 1969. Reflections on the ability dimension in human society. In B.C. Rosen, H.J. Crockett & C.Z. Nunn (Eds.), *Achievement in American Society* (pp. 18 - 32). Cambridge, Mass.: Schenkman Publishing Company, Inc.

Kluckhohn, C. 1949. *Mirror for Man*. New York: McGraw Hill.

MacKinnon, D.W. 1965. Personality correlates of creativity. In M.J. Ashner & C.E. Bish (Eds.), *Productive Thinking in Education* (pp. 159 - 171). New York: The National Education Association.

Maslow, A. 1976. Creativity in self-actualizing people. In A. Rothenberg & C.R. Hausman (Eds.), *The Creativity Question* (pp. 86 - 92). Durham, NC: Duke University Press.

Rosen, B.C., Crockett, H.J. & Nunn, C.Z. 1969. Introduction. In B.C. Rosen, H.J. Crockett & C.Z. Nunn (Eds.), *Achievement in American Society* (pp. 3 - 8). Cambridge, Mass.: Schenkman Publishing Company, Inc.

Rosenberg, M. 1979. *Conceiving The Self*. New York: Basic Books.

Shekerjian, D. 1990. *Uncommon Genius*. New York: Viking.

Tieger, P.D. & Barron-Tieger, B. 1995. *Do What You Are*. Second edition. New York: Little, Brown and Company.

Yount, K. 1986. A theory of productive activity: The relationships among self-concept, gender, sex-role stereotypes, and work-emergent traits. *Psychology of Women Quarterly* **10** : 63 - 88

172 Portraits of Excellence

List of Symbols

a	acceleration
A	attitude (ASK MET PF)
d	diameter of particle conduit
D	diameter of relevant group
E	equipment (ASK MET PF)
F	force
F	social fund (ASK MET PF)
h	particle position
I	current
K	knowledge (ASK MET PF)
m	mass
M	money (ASK MET PF)
P	people (ASK MET PF)
pd	potential difference
R	resistance
S	skills (ASK MET PF)
t	time
T	time (ASK MET PF)
U	initial velocity
V	velocity (final)
V_t	terminal velocity
η_{ar}	need to avoid reality
η_{bv}	breadth of view
η_{ee}	need for emotional expression
η_{fo}	need for others
η_{go}	need to be greater than others
η_{sd}	need for self-defense
η_{sr}	speed of response to motivation
φ_p	particle momentum
λ_p	particle sphericity

Index

abundance 157-158
Achebe 19
achievement 14, 83, 96, 140, 154 - 158, 166, 167
adventurous 102, 106
aggravation 161-162
aggression 78 - 86, 162
alcoholism 60, 63 - 64, 162
anger 21, 80, 89, 90, 92
appetite 89, 107, 109
approval 70, 71, 107, 108, 125
Aristotle 65, 126, 136
Aronson 66, 73, 148
aspiration 16, 156, 159
assertive 105, 169
attitude 118, 121 - 125, 146, 157, 167, 167-170

bankruptcy 82
Barron-Tieger 69
beauty 141, 147 - 148
Behan 140
Bennett 143
bias 35 - 36
biology 26, 37
Blake 142
blame 43, 47, 104, 106
body language 45, 107, 132
boil 89
Boileau-Despreaux 141
bold 11, 102, 106 - 107
breadth 49, 52, 58, 101
breakthrough 135, 136
Brown 142
brutality 156
bulwark 139, 140, 147
Butler 5

Carver 31
caution 64, 88, 90, 103, 108, 129, 146
city 50
classification 11 - 12, 101 - 102
communication skills 131 - 134
companions 15 - 16
competition 48, 78 - 86, 145, 154 -157, 169
compliments 67, 70
conformity 72, 124, 149, 162
considerate 42, 43, 47, 49, 50, 109
Cook 144
cope 8, 60, 62
crave 5, 63, 64, 68
creativity 49, 110, 144, 156
crime 83, 85, 170
critical frustration level 88, 89, 92
Crockett 14
culture 15, 123 - 124
cunningness 40, 45, 48, 155
curiosity 12, 13, 50 - 53, 57

deep self 19, 51
design 6, 7, 36, 170
devotion 94, 98, 99, 159
Dickens 141
discipline 127
drive 13, 18, 24, 27, 29, 95
drug abuse 60, 63, 64
drugs 106, 107, 162, 169
dynamic impulsiveness 95 - 96, 100

easy-going 102, 105
education 51, 137, 138
Einstein 19
Emerson 131, 136
emotional control 88, 89, 92, 107
emotional expression 31, 87, 88, 101
empowerment 9, 32, 58, 111, 115-118, 167, 168
engineering 7, 9, 19, 37, 170
environment 13, 26, 32, 33, 37, 166, 167, 169
envy 79, 84, 158
equipment 118, 122, 125, 143, 158, 168
excellence 5 - 8, 127, 142
external control 67, 73, 75
extraversion 68 - 74, 102 - 103, 108

faking 40, 46, 48
fame 106, 159
family 71, 90, 107, 108, 122, 125, 126, 137, 141, 144
fantasy 60 - 62, 64
fashion 63
Fielding 141
fortune 159
fortune-tellers 61
frame of reference 34
friction 21 - 22
fulfillment 14, 15, 17, 19, 22, 128
fuse 88

gambling 60, 62, 63
gender 147, 149
giftedness 14, 15, 144, 146
global planning 50, 54, 57

gossip 60, 64
grooming 107
group-orientedness 67
guilt 43, 47
gurus 61, 162

hallucinations 162
hate 17, 44, 47, 158, 162
health 17, 18, 129 - 130
helplessness 21, 25, 61,143, 149, 162
Herodotus 144
Hesiod 127
holier-than-thou 79
hostile 22, 61, 162
human mind 5, 70, 81
human nature 6, 8, 20, 37
Human Resources 20

idealistic 92
immigrants 158
impersonal 6, 19, 36
impulsive 95 - 99, 109, 110
inconsideration 40
indecisive 90 - 91
initiative 93, 96, 97, 99
innovative 135
interdependency 17
intimidation 169
introversion 45, 68, 103 - 108

jealousy 79, 84
Jesus Christ 19
justice 79, 170

Kluckhohn 124
knowledge 12 - 15, 20, 21, 52, 118, 121, 125, 126, 135 - 139, 150, 158, 167

life Skills   126
listening   132
local planning   50, 54, 57
looking glass   23, 34 - 37
Lord Beaverbrook   128
Lord Halifax   146

magic   13, 138, 169
map   36, 37
Marx   19
Maslow   45
Maugham   139
metaphors   8, 56
Miller   34, 146
mirror   7, 8, 35
money   70, 118, 21, 124, 125, 129, 139 - 151, 158, 167, 168
motivation   31, 93, 100, 116, 118, 153 - 159
Myers-Briggs   69

naive   45, 48, 110
narrow-view   49, 50, 53, 54
nonconformism   72 - 73
Nunn   14

open   50, 52
optimists   56, 91
order   50, 55 - 57

party   67, 71, 75, 103, 107
Pascal   136
patience   131
perfectionistic   92
performance   37, 166 - 167
perseverance   100, 131, 162
persistent devotion   94
philosophers   6
physics   7, 9, 170

picture   33, 36, 37, 50 - 56
Plato   19, 124
portrait   6, 7, 8, 33, 36
potential difference   24 - 27, 30, 39, 40, 66, 87 - 89, 154, 155, 158
poverty   141 - 144, 150, 158, 159
power   108, 135, 138, 141, 144, 156, 159, 169
praise   67, 70, 75, 107, 109, 156, 159
prejudice   18, 22, 47, 83 - 85, 170
prestige   103, 108
problem-solving skills   129
promiscuity   162
psychics   61, 162
psychological testing   15
Publilius Syrus   128

race   22, 44, 83, 124, 147 - 149, 169, 170
reckless   62, 106, 162, 164
recognition   159
reform   166 - 167
relationships   15, 70, 105, 106, 109, 130, 141, 144, 145, 166, 169
research   46, 53, 166
Riis   131
risk   59, 60, 129, 130, 141, 144, 162
romance   67, 74, 75, 89
Rosen   14
Rosenberg   124
Rousseau   20

Scheier   31
science   7, 13, 16, 25, 35, 36

secretive 45, 47, 104
self-actualization 5, 144
self-confidence 7, 56, 58, 91, 96
self-control 88, 89, 91
self-esteem 91, 121 - 125, 149, 157, 165, 167
self-orientedness 40
self-positioning 133
self-presentation 133
self-sufficiency 56, 69, 74
selfishness 41, 42, 48 - 50, 78, 110, 155, 156, 162
sensation 62, 106, 107, 108
sex 67, 74, 75, 89, 106, 107, 109, 124, 147, 149
Shakespeare 133
Shaw 72, 142
Shekerjian 150
shrewd 45, 108
singleness of purpose 93, 97 - 98
skills 25, 52, 62, 118, 121, 126, 165 - 170
social engineering 7, 19
social fund 118, 122, 126, 146 - 151, 157, 158
social image 71
social justice 166, 170
social processing 67, 72, 162
status quo 50, 53, 57
Stockdale 139
stress 21, 60, 62
subtlety 45, 48, 104
success 83, 86, 106, 127, 131, 140, 142, 155, 156
suspicious 44, 102, 105

tact 40, 45, 104 - 105, 132
talents 7, 128, 156
temper tantrums 90
Thoreau 144
thrill 62, 63, 64, 106
Tieger 69
time 20, 118, 122, 128, 143, 144, 158
trait 30, 31, 32, 40, 46, 48, 79, 83, 91
treating people 169
trickery 110
trustworthy 109

vanity 60, 62, 63, 64
vigilant 104
vindictive 44, 47, 105, 106
violence 22, 83
visionary 103, 109 - 110
Voltaire 141
vulnerable 25, 39, 40, 42, 44, 84

war 21 - 22
waste 20, 21, 135
weakness 44, 46, 128
wealth 19, 158, 159
Webster 133
well-rounded 73, 75
wickedness 81, 83, 86, 110, 162
Wilcox 130
Wilde 140

Yount 165

zeal 16, 95, 98